1(

MW01156480

101 Coaching Strategies and Techniques provides focused, practical strategies to help the coach with their work. Each point provides a detailed explanation of the strategy together with potential pitfalls and solutions.

Contributors from a range of coaching backgrounds are brought together to cover a number of issues faced by professional coaches including:

- confidence building
- developing specific skills and strategies
- group coaching
- problem solving and creativity
- self awareness
- the stuck client.

101 Coaching Strategies and Techniques will be a handy reference tool for busy coaches; the bite-sized strategies will also provide a useful guide for those in training.

Gladeana McMahon is Fellow and Chair of the Association for Coaching, UK. Her publications include *Achieving Excellence in Your Coaching Practice* and *Essential Skills for Setting up a Counselling or Psychotherapy Practice*. Gladeana was listed as one of the UK's 'top ten coaches' in the *Independent on Sunday*.

Anne Archer develops leadership and change capability in organisations in both the public and private sector. She also facilitates coach training programmes, open and in-house, and provides 1:1 and group supervision. Anne works with leaders and coaches across the globe. She is Editor of the Association for Coaching bulletin and is a member of the ICF.

Essential Coaching Skills and Knowledge
Series Editors: Gladeana McMahon,
Stephen Palmer & Averil Leimon

The **Essential Coaching Skills and Knowledge** series provides an accessible and lively introduction to key areas in the developing field of coaching. Each title in the series is written by leading coaches with extensive experience and has a strong practical emphasis, including illustrative vignettes, summary boxes, exercises and activities. Assuming no prior knowledge, these books will appeal to professionals in business, management, human resources, psychology, counselling and psychotherapy, as well as students and tutors of coaching and coaching psychology.

www.routledgementalhealth.com/essential-coaching-skills

Titles in the series:

Essential Business Coaching
Averil Leimon, François Moscovici & Gladeana McMahon

**Achieving Excellence in Your Coaching Practice:
How to Run a Highly Successful Coaching Business**
Gladeana McMahon, Stephen Palmer & Christine Wilding

**A Guide to Coaching and Mental Health: The
Recognition and Management of Psychological Issues**
Andrew Buckley & Carole Buckley

Essential Life Coaching Skills
Angela Dunbar

101 Coaching Strategies and Techniques
Edited by Gladeana McMahon & Anne Archer

Group and Team Coaching: The Essential Guide
Christine Thornton

The Coaching Relationship: Putting People First
Stephen Palmer & Almuth McDowall

101 Coaching Strategies and Techniques

Edited by Gladeana McMahon and Anne Archer

Routledge
Taylor & Francis Group

LONDON AND NEW YORK

First published 2010
by Routledge
27 Church Lane, Hove, East Sussex BN3 2FA

Simultaneously published in the USA and Canada
by Routledge
270 Madison Avenue, New York NY 10016

Reprinted 2010

Routledge is an imprint of the Taylor & Francis Group, an Informa business

© 2010 Selection and editorial matter, Gladeana McMahon and
Anne Archer; individual chapters, the contributors

Typeset in New Century Schoolbook by
RefineCatch Limited, Bungay, Suffolk
Printed and bound in Great Britain by
TJ International Ltd, Padstow, Cornwall
Paperback cover design by Lisa Dynan

This publication has been produced with paper manufactured to strict
environmental standards and with pulp derived from sustainable forests.

British Library Cataloguing in Publication Data
A catalogue record for this book is available from the British Library

Library of Congress Cataloging-in-Publication Data
101 coaching strategies and techniques / edited by Gladeana McMahon &
Anne Archer.
    p. cm.
    ISBN 978–0–415–47333–0 (hbk.) – ISBN 978–0–415–47334–7 (pbk.)
1. Personal coaching. 2. Executive coaching. 3. Counselling–Practice.
I. McMahon, Gladeana, 1954– II. Archer, Anne, 1960– III. Title: 101 coaching
strategies and techniques.
    BF637.P36A15 2010
    158′.3–dc22

                                                                    2009040663

ISBN: 978–0–415–47333–0 (hbk)
ISBN: 978–0–415–47334–7 (pbk)

Contents

List of figures and tables

Figures

Tables

List of Contributors

David Adams is a business and leadership coach working with individuals and groups. A chartered accountant, and a former chief executive officer of a major stockbroker, he runs groups for Vistage, the world's leading chief executive membership organization. He is an accredited member of the Association for Coaching and an international performance poet. david@dhadams.co.uk

Anne Archer works with individuals and organizations from the public and private sector to develop resourceful and resilient leaders. She has worked in the United States and Europe and has coached clients from the United States, Australia, South Africa, India, Europe, Canada and New Zealand. www.annearcherassociates.com

Caroline Shola Arewa has transformed lives using Health and Success Coaching for over 20 years. She is author of three books and numerous articles, a humanistic psychologist and yoga master. Shola trained practitioners in complementary medicine for 10 years and is currently a spiritual coaching trainer. She also directs Energy 4 Life. www.shola.co.uk

Elspeth Campbell is an organizational consultant, and an Association for Coaching accredited executive coach and supervisor with cross-sector experience from management consultancy. She is a skilled communicator with a deep understanding of human issues, and is qualified in psychology and psychometric testing. Elspeth has an MSc in Systemic Management and her coaching strategies represent systemic organizational practice. elspeth@ozten.demon.co.uk

Christine K. Champion is founder of Acumen Executive Coaching Ltd and an Associate on the Masters Programme in Coaching and Mentoring at Oxford Brookes University. An experienced, accredited executive coach and coaching supervisor, with an MBA from Henley, Christine sees coaching as a tool situated at the heart of organizational strategy. ckc@acumen-executive.com

Heather Cooper is Director of executive coaching at Gordon Cooper Associates, and runs the online 360-degree analysis company Executive Coaching Tools. Both companies design bespoke management development, executive coaching and 360-degree solutions to help individuals, teams and organizations perform. Heather can be contacted via www.gordoncooper.co.uk   or www.executivecoachingtools.co.uk

Julia Cusack is a leadership development consultant and executive coach, and has worked for GCHQ and Bridge Consulting. Her attention to the significance and use of words features extensively in her coaching practice. She is also a graduate and associate faculty member of the Academy of Executive Coaching's Advanced Diploma programme. www.juliacusack.co.uk

Gill Dickers is an experienced leadership and corporate coach and trainer. She offers a fresh and flexible approach using a range of creative techniques to promote change. She has extensive experience and has developed and delivered many successful courses in public, charity and voluntary agencies. www.gdcoaching.co.uk

Angela Dunbar is an accredited coach, and council member of the Association for Coaching, nominated for 'Influencing Service to the Profession of Coaching' and 'Impacting Service to the Wider Community' AC Honorary Awards in 2008. Angela specializes in Clean Language and Emergent Knowledge. www.angeladunbar.co.uk

Denis Gorce-Bourge is a corporate coach, psychotherapist, NLP master and practitioner in hypnosis, TLT, EFT and visualization. He specializes in emotional, stress-related issues and change management. He runs conferences and workshops for corporate and private clients in England and abroad. His professional accreditations are at www.gblifecoaching.co.uk

Bruce Grimley is a chartered occupational psychologist, accredited coach and NLP trainer. He is an assessor for the British Psychological Society Level A psychometric courses and original founding council member of the Association for Coaching (AC). He initiated the current AC competency framework. Bruce is an Associate Fellow of the British Psychological Society and coaches from an NLP perspective. www.achieving-lives.co.uk; www.innergame.co.uk

Gill Hicks is a personal communications specialist. As a coach and trainer, she works to develop outstanding interpersonal skills leading to a powerful professional impact and greater confidence. She has over 20 years' experience across many industry sectors. She is an NLP master practitioner, coach and member of the Association for Coaching. gill@gillhicks.co.uk

Diana Hogbin-Mills is a director at Talentmax. She is Head of Research for the Association for Coaching, a Fellow of the RSA and affiliate of the CIPD. She is an accredited coach, an NLP practitioner and has a degree in Psychology. She regularly writes and speaks on talent and career issues. www.talentmax.co.uk

Mags McGeever is a life enthusiast and professional coach. She enjoys working with a wide variety of clients on a range of issues and is also an accredited advanced confidence coach. Her background is in law, where she gained a 1st-class degree, and worked in both commercial practice and academia before moving into coaching. hello@magsmcgeever.com

Gladeana McMahon is director of professional coaching standards for Cedar TM. She is Fellow and Chair of the

Association for Coaching, and Fellow of the British Association for Counselling and Psychotherapy, Institute of Management Specialists and Royal Society of Arts. www.gladeanamcmahon.com

Peter Melrose is an experienced independent executive coach who works with large corporate organizations at senior level. He spent 13 years in the Hay Group where he was a director and shareholder. He is an associate member of the British Psychological Society, a member of the International Coach Federation (ICF) and holds a Master Coach qualification from the Academy of Executive Coaching (AoEC). peter.melrose@blueyonder.co.uk

Joan O'Connor is an executive coach, group facilitator and consultant in leadership development. Qualified in different coaching disciplines, she takes an integrated approach to her work, encouraging individuals to achieve positive, sustainable change. Joan practices through her own business, is an associate for Cedar TM, and an advisor to The Writer. Joan@thinkpurple.co.uk

Darryl Stevens is an advanced accredited executive coach (ICF accredited programme) with over 15 years' senior experience with global organizations and a degree in international business management. He blends multi-discipline and multi-sector leadership experience with psychology and coaching mastery. He has ongoing connections with Harvard University and is Assistant Faculty on the Academy of Executive Coaching Advanced Diploma Programme. darryl.stevens@aoec.com

Penny Swinburne has over 20 years' UK and international experience, across diverse sectors, of executive and personal development coaching, managing coaching contracts and training coaches. She is a chartered psychologist, founder member of the Association of Business Psychologists and a member of the Chartered Institute of Personnel and Development. penny@psa1.fsnet.co.uk

Aidan Tod's added value is in facilitating individuals and teams to achieve their objectives faster and to higher quality than they would have done on their own. Aidan uses his extensive experience of people, organizations and change in international human resources with blue-chip and government organizations to do this. www.12exec.co.uk

Helen Warner is an independent executive and leadership coach. She is a member of the Association for Coaching and a graduate member of the Chartered Institute of Personnel and Development. She has a Foundation Certificate in Family Therapy and has an honours degree in Experimental Psychology. www.abbeywarner.com

Introduction

We hope you find this book a useful addition to your book-case. By bringing together the expertise of a number of experienced coaches, this book aims to provide you with additional strategies and exercises to add to your coaching toolkit. We hope you will find that this is the type of book you can refer back to time and time again.

What this book is and what it is not

This book is meant to be a resource that provides a variety of exercises, techniques and strategies that have proven helpful to the coaches who have contributed them. They are used by the contributors in their day-to-day coaching work with individuals, teams and organizations. You will see that many of the exercises have been adapted by the coaches concerned from exercises and strategies from the world of psychology, business and education.

This book is not meant to be an academic book; it does not seek to provide the reader with the latest research or go into detailed academic depth on any given topic. Nor does it aim to provide a definitive list of strategies or be a book about coaching theory, models or skills.

The aim of this book is to provide readers with a resource that can be dipped in and out of when seeking to add additional practical strategies to an existing coaching toolkit.

How is the book organized?

The book is organized into sections that cover a range of common issues faced by coaches:

- confidence building
- developing as a coach
- developing specific skills and strategies
- focusing on the future
- group coaching
- problem solving and creativity
- relationships
- self awareness
- when the client gets stuck.

Whilst each section has a number of strategies, we have kept the format the same for ease of reference. However, the style and content will vary according to the style of the individual coach. If you want to contact any one of the contributors, their details are provided in the list of contributors.

Government health warning

Whilst having a range of strategies and techniques available to use for the range of clients and client issues that are often presented in coaching can help clients achieve their goals, such strategies and techniques are only an aid to assist the coaching process. Building a sound coaching alliance and being able to assess individual client needs ensures a holistic, tailor-made offering to the client. When coaching relies solely on strategies and techniques without these being integrated into a coaching model, there is a danger that the process becomes technique rather than client centred.

A

Confidence building

A strengths and skills exercise

Gill Dickers

Purpose

This exercise is aimed at building a sense of self. From a position of strength, the client will be more able to state their own goals and dreams, rather than being preoccupied with the expectations of others.

Description

During an individual coaching session, a client may repeatedly use words like 'ought', 'should' and 'would'. This can suggest that they are doing something to please other people, or that they think other people want them to behave in particular ways. For example, new students may be doing a course of study to please their teachers or family.

Process

There are three steps to this strategy:

- **Step 1: Self-confidence**
  To promote self-confidence, ask your client to talk about a *past experience* or *achievement* they are proud of. Often when people talk about past successes, their posture becomes more upright, they breathe more deeply, they smile and look relaxed. Give positive feedback about this, ensuring that you are congruent with the praise you offer.

- **Step 2: Explore the concept of success**
  Based on the experience they offer you, ask the coachee how their senses are stimulated by success. How does success smell, how does it feel, what colour is it, does it have a texture, can they draw it? Discuss the strengths and skills they have demonstrated.
- **Step 3: Devise a positive list**
  Before the next session, ask the client to make a list of all the positive things about themselves they can think of, with the number on the list being equivalent to their age. So, if your client is 25 years old, he or she composes a list of 25 things: this will further encourage their self-confidence.

Pitfalls

If the client has very low self-esteem and is depressed, the exercise may be inappropriate or too challenging.

Achieving an outcome by exploring metaphors

Angela Dunbar

Purpose

Most coaching processes begin with setting a clear outcome. This exercise is slightly different in that we are encouraging the client to set an outcome using metaphoric language to aid getting a deeper, more fundamental goal to motivate the client to action. This exercise belongs to what is referred to as 'Clean Language'.

Description

You can ask a Clean Language question to encourage the client to set an outcome. The question is: 'What would you like to have happen?'. You can ask this question at the outset of a coaching session, or you could ask it at any point during a session when the client describes a real or perceived problem in metaphor. To help the client stay in their metaphoric thinking, repeat their description of the problem back to them just before the question. For example, 'And when you are banging your head against a brick wall, what would you like to have happen?'.

Process

If you ask the question at the beginning of a session and you get a logical, non-metaphoric answer like: 'I want to get that promotion', you can explore the outcome using the two questions given in the strategy 'Noticing and paying attention to metaphors' (p. 232), paying attention to any metaphoric descriptions they may use to describe the outcome.

Just because you ask for an outcome, it doesn't mean you'll get one. Quite often you'll get a re-statement of the problem such as: 'I just don't seem to be making progress'.

As above, repeat their summary of the problem (and the metaphoric description if they have given one) and repeat the question 'What would you like to have happen?'. Sometimes the client will answer the question by stating a 'remedy' rather than an actual outcome. So, rather than an end result, the client describes a proposed solution that they think will help them move forward. For example, 'I'd like to break through the wall and find a path'. Or, they say they would like to reduce or remove the problem, whatever it is. For instance, an outcome of 'I'd like to stop smoking', in this context, would be considered a proposed remedy rather than an actual outcome.

Ask the client, what would happen next if they were to achieve their proposed remedy. This is likely to get you a real (and more motivating) outcome. Here's the phrasing of the Clean Language question (once again start with a repetition of the client's description):

Coach: And when you break through the wall and find a path, then what happens?
Client: Then I can finally get to a place where I can just be myself, and be happy.

This sounds like an outcome, so once again you can start to explore it with the two simple Clean Language questions above.

Any time the client gives you a problem, repeat their description of the problem and ask: 'What would you like to have happen?'. Any time the client gives you a remedy, repeat their description of the remedy and ask: 'Then what happens?'. This exercise is used often enough for a client to get a real sense of the outcome, the problems that have been stopping them achieving the outcome so far and what strategies will/will not work to get them there.

The exercise and the questioning can be carried out without a special focus on metaphors; however, it is much,

much more powerful if you focus your questions and attention in this way. By doing so you help bypass the client's ability to block or censor their answers as metaphors hold a different meaning than simple statements.

Like many coaching strategies, this one works on the basis of concentrating the client's attention on where they want to be, away from what's stopping them. This different, positive perspective is usually motivating and refreshing for the client.

Pitfalls

Depending on the problem or issue the client is working with, they may find it very difficult to give a clear outcome. Some clients are so hypnotized by the problem that they find it very difficult to talk about anything else. Some clients are stuck in a bind. By wanting whatever it is they want, this creates a conflict that in itself creates the problem. In this situation, the client won't automatically move forward with this exercise, but it might help you to identify and understand their 'stuckness'.

Bibliography

Tompkins, P. and Lawley, J. (2000) *Metaphors in Mind*, London: The Developing Company Press.

Tompkins, P. and Lawley, J. (2006) *Coaching for P.R.O.s* (*Coach the Coach*, February edition), Littleport: Fenman.

3

Acting positively in difficult situations

Penny Swinburne

Purpose

Many outwardly confident and able people lack confidence in particular situations. Examples include: 'fast trackers' who may say nothing at meetings because everyone else there is 'older', 'wiser' and perhaps 'male' (often said by young women) and are scared of 'looking foolish'; and specialists, whose training leads them to be confident only when they 'know the answer for sure'. This exercise helps the client to break the negative cycle of lack of confidence leading to ineffective action that has built up, and to replace it with positive action.

Description

The exercise enables the client to identify the negative thoughts they habitually engage in and how these link to ineffective action. It then shows ways of breaking the negative cycle, by replacing the negative thoughts with positive thoughts, which then enable the person to manage the negative feelings that the thought process created. The exercise has its roots in cognitive-behavioural coaching and is a simple version borrowed from assertiveness training.

Process

Write on a flip chart the hierarchy Situation, Thoughts, Feelings, Actions with regard to a situation relevant to the client, as shown in Figure 1. Here we are using the example of contributing to meetings.

Then work through the hierarchy, asking the client relevant questions at each level, writing their answers to the right. For example, 'What sorts of thoughts go through your mind in these meetings?' ('Well, that they all know far more than me; if I say anything, I'll look foolish'); 'How do you feel?' ('I feel unconfident and anxious'); 'As a result, how do you act?' ('I don't say anything'). The client will then begin to realise the negative, self-defeating cycle they engage in – this can be represented on the flip chart by drawing arrows through the written answers from thoughts, to feelings, to actions and from actions back to the thoughts.

Then move to two ways of breaking the cycle:

- **Breaking the negative thought**
  You may ask the client: 'If you took the negative voice out of your head, what positive thoughts could you play to yourself that would be realistic?'. The client may respond by stating: 'I bring a different perspective'; 'I wouldn't have been asked if I had nothing to contribute'. Write on the left of the cycle, following through with similar questions at the levels of feelings and actions, to show a positive, reinforcing cycle, similarly completed with arrows.

Figure 1 **The negative cycle**

- **Breaking the negative feelings**
  Encourage the client to practise consciously setting their non-verbal behaviour to be confident – supported by consciously relaxing muscles and breathing deeply. In a short time, the feelings will follow the non-verbal behaviour.

You can encourage your client to practise this exercise along a continuum of difficult situations, for example starting with contributing at a less important meeting and moving to more difficult ones. You can suggest that they ask a trusted person to give them feedback when they try the new behaviour.

Pitfalls

Some people are sceptical about the power of positive thinking. It can help to say that positive thoughts need to be believable, not just wishful thinking. Occasionally, negative thoughts are recognized from childhood or other situations. Be prepared to recognize this, but you don't have to go there.

Bibliography

Adapted from: Beck, A. T. (1976) *Cognitive Therapy and the Emotional Disorders*, New York, NY: International Universities Press.

4

Building general confidence and self-esteem

Penny Swinburne

Purpose

This exercise (whose origin is lost in the mists of time for me) can be used independently of the coaching session, where there is a real lack of self-confidence. It can be done between coaching sessions and then followed up at a subsequent coaching session.

Description

The client is invited to write lists of different types of positives from their lives and to repeat three items at a time to themselves until they believe them. A tiny investment of time in this exercise, which can be done alongside other daily activities, can be fun and have big pay-offs.

Process

The guidance you give to your client is as follows. 'Write lists of:

- 10 achievements;
- 10 things you do well;
- 10 things you like about your body.'

You need to be very encouraging as for some people it will be hard to list 10 things so encourage them to capture as many as possible. Alternatively, you could be selective of which lists the client compiles as people often find the third particularly challenging, but then that can be a good reason for trying to do it. You may need to be careful to explain what 'achievements' mean to some people. For example, it doesn't have to be a major event. The example I use is passing my driving test (yes, therein lies a story), which also helps to keep it light. Likewise, 'things you do well' can be *anything* – making cakes, scoring goals etc. You could rephrase this as 'things you seem to do more easily than others'.

You then encourage your client to take any three items from these lists and suggest that they repeat them especially when they have dead time on their hands, for example when in a traffic jam, in the bath or on a bus. Once the client feels comfortable with these three items then they can move on to another three from the lists.

The selling point of this exercise is not the particular issues themselves but rather a gradual building up of a good self-picture and confidence in this.

At the next coaching session, you can check out how it's going. It's also sometimes useful to get them to say out loud to you one or two items from their lists. For example, 'I am good at making cakes/scoring goals'. You can give feedback on the confidence/assertiveness shown in their words and non-verbal behaviour. Once you have started them off, the process usually becomes self-supporting.

Pitfalls

Some people will be highly sceptical of this exercise. I find it's usually best not to be too serious (helped by my own examples of where the exercise has helped) and to offer it on a 'you've got nothing to lose' basis. As in the previous exercise, occasionally it can take people back to childhood issues or other past difficult situations. Again, be prepared to recognize this, but you don't have to go there.

Bibliography

Jeffers, S. (1999) *The Little Book of Confidence*, London: Rider & Co.
McMahon, G. (2000) *Confidence Works: Learn to Be your Own Life Coach*, London: Sheldon Press.

5

Celebration and reward

Mags McGeever

Purpose

This exercise is about the celebration of and reward for
achieving a goal or a step along the way to it, which plays a
significant role in the coaching process. A client may not be
in the habit of celebrating their achievements or feeling
proud of themselves and may even find this quite difficult.
In today's busy world it is very easy for someone to get
used to achieving a goal and moving straight onto the next
thing on their list without pausing for reflection or perhaps
even noticing what they have done, never mind praising
themselves for it.

Description

For a good coaching experience, the emphasis will not only
be on achieving a goal but also on ensuring that the journey
is a joy. Hopefully the client, together with the coach, will
have come up with some ideas for making the route to their
goal an enjoyable process in itself but, to enhance this
enjoyment, celebrations of varying size at various stages
along the route are very important.

   Rewards are also relevant here and can be used in con-
junction with celebration to further strengthen the process.
The promise of a special treat is not only a good way of
motivating a client towards their goals but also a method of
providing evidence for their success in achieving that goal.

Process

- Assist the client in coming up with a SMART goal (specific, measurable, achievable, realistic and time-bound).
- Then work with the client through the rest of the GROW or other coaching model being used until they have come up with the actions they will take towards their goal.
- Through effective questioning and listening, ascertain how keen the client is to take those actions. Actions that they are not so excited about (yet are still suitable for achieving the goal they truly want) may require greater or more frequent rewards in order to incentivize and motivate the client.
- Do check with the client whether including a reward appeals to them (perhaps doing the action is reward enough).
- Ask the client what they will do to celebrate once they achieve their goal. And who will they celebrate with – alone, with friends or family, with you as their coach? Do remember that the coaching relationship may be the only place where the client feels they can acknowledge their successes in this way without judgement by others.
- Use creative questioning to come up with fabulous juicy rewards that really mean something to the client. This will be ever so personal to each individual – something very basic for one person may be an indulgent luxury for another. This might involve taking the client back to a time when they were more carefree or had more time for themselves or running them through a visualization of their perfect day and then using some of the elements they describe. Get creative!
- Make sure it is clear when the reward is due so that the client has something specific to work towards.

In a later session:

- Ask the client how they got on with their proposed actions.
- For those they have already achieved, congratulate them. Ask them how they felt when they achieved them. Ask them how they feel now they are telling you about it. If the client becomes more aware of the positive feelings that are

engendered they will automatically be more likely to complete future actions as they will have a more positive experience in their mind.

- If any actions have not been taken, in addition to other coaching methods (such as assessing obstacles, and whether the actions or indeed the goal are appropriate) remind the client of the reward they will engage in once they have reached a certain point. Working to their predominant preference (depending on whether the person is predominantly visual, auditory or kinaesthetic), ask the client what they are looking forward to about that reward, how they will feel when they get/do it, what they will see, what they will hear, what they will taste, etc.

Pitfalls

Some clients may feel truly uncomfortable in acknowledging or rewarding themselves in this way. Try to ascertain whether this is just a behaviour they are not used to but are willing to learn. If that is not the case, it may be a good idea to use sensitive questioning and exercises to help them build their self-esteem until they become more comfortable with treating themselves really well. You can then use the concept of celebration and reward to great effect!

Bibliography

Ready, R. (2004) *Neuro-Linguistic Programming for Dummies*, Hoboken, NJ: John Wiley & Sons.
Whitmore, J. (1998) *Coaching for Performance* (2nd edition), London: Nicholas Brealey Publishing.

6

Coping imagery

Gladeana McMahon

Purpose

This exercise aims to help the client increase his/her ability
to cope with difficult and/or challenging situations. It is a
stress-proofing exercise that helps to increase psychological
resilience.

Description

Once the coaching relationship is established, the client is
provided with a rationale as to why it may be useful to use
coping imagery as a strategy to assist in the management of
the difficult situation that s/he is facing, for example, if s/he
needs to prepare for an important presentation, difficult
team meeting or an interview.

The rationale behind using coping imagery is that if the
client can imagine him or herself dealing with a situation by
visualizing it, this provides an opportunity of practising the
range of coping strategies that are discussed in the coaching
session in a safe environment with the coach. By doing this,
the client gets an opportunity of trying out such strategies
using his/her imagination and, as a by-product, also gets the
opportunity of experiencing a sense of control when s/he is
able to deal with a situation effectively. It also offers the
opportunity of fine tuning the coping strategies to be used by
the client, should the client discover problems in applying
these while imagining dealing with the situation in question.

This exercise can also be used as a tool to help the client

to imagine a different future that might involve significant change, for example, if the individual is faced with taking up a new role within an organization. The coach can also refer back to the research available in the psychological arena that supports the premise of 'role rehearsal' and how, by imagining a successful outcome, such an outcome is more likely to be achieved.

Process

When being used as a tool for dealing with a difficult situation, the client is asked to sit comfortably and imagine the situation that is causing the difficulty. S/he is then encouraged to visualize the situation. For example, if the client is concerned about giving a major presentation, s/he is asked to imagine who would be there, the sights, sounds, smells, layout of the room and the presentation that is to be given. S/he is then encouraged to imagine what coping strategies (including any that have been discussed in the session, such as breathing exercises) could be used and to imagine the presentation taking place successfully. When the client is able to imagine a positive outcome, this provides a sense of emotional control over the situation and the degree of difficulty can be increased. For example, the client could imagine giving the presentation in a calm manner and then imagine that a person in the audience is looking bored or asks a question and how s/he would cope with this. It is important to encourage the client to visualize all aspects of the situation from arriving to give the presentation, setting up the room, seeing the audience and how they are reacting to the presentation to dealing with any concerns s/he might have of challenging situations that could arise.

Once the client has successfully completed this exercise in the coaching session, s/he can practise the exercise as a homework assignment.

Pitfalls

There are normally no associated pitfalls with this exercise.

Bibliography

Palmer, S. and Dryden, W. (1995) *Counselling for Stress Problems*, London: Sage Publications.

7

Creating a stronger feeling of confidence (or any other positive feeling or resource) using Clean Language

Angela Dunbar

Purpose

This is an exercise to help a client gain more understanding of how they access their own confidence, so that they are able to access it more effectively in the future, either consciously or subconsciously. The exercise is the easiest one to demonstrate the positive effects of Clean Language. It's quite easy for the facilitator too, as it has a clear process.

Description

This is an excellent, standalone example of how you can use Clean Language in a specific context, that is, helping a client to develop a resource of some kind. An often requested resource is 'more confidence'.

Process

First, ask a few simple Clean Language questions to explore 'confidence' with the client (see the strategy 'Noticing and paying attention to metaphors' on p. 232). Once you have a good description (and maybe started to evoke the feeling in the client, from their concentration on it), ask a question to find a location for the confidence – all feelings have a physical location somewhere in the body. Repeat back a few of the client's descriptive words about confidence and ask the question in the following way:

- 'And when confidence is warm and glowing, *whereabouts* is that warm glowing confidence?'

Hopefully, the client will point somewhere around their body. It's worth asking this question again to pinpoint a more exact location:

- 'And when that warm, glowing confidence is there in your heart, *whereabouts* in your heart is that?'

The next question to ask is one to bring the resource to life:

- 'And when that warm, glowing confidence is right there in the centre of your heart, does that confidence have a *size or a shape*?'

You may need to ask a few more simple Clean Language questions to help develop their awareness of some kind of object or mass. At this point the client might spontaneously give you a metaphor for it. If not, you have another question you can ask:

- **'And when confidence is small, round and glowing in your heart, that's small and round like what?'**

Ask the question very slowly, particularly the last few words. This will normally have the result of the client now expressing their resource as a metaphor, now with a location somewhere inside them or nearby. This is already a really useful way to help the client be able to access the resource.

To help them get even more of it, you could use two approaches: (a) achieve an outcome – ask them what they'd like to have happen (in connection with a problem they have stated regarding their confidence); or (b) you could move things on in time, which often means the resource grows spontaneously. Here's the Clean Language question to ask:

- 'And when that small, round ball of fire in your heart is glowing, then what happens?'

You can keep going forward, asking 'Then what happens?'

and 'What happens next?', exploring all the metaphors the client uses along the way. To end the session, you may ask:

- 'And as we bring this exercise to an end, what do you know now about your confidence?'

Pitfalls

Some clients find the 'whereabouts' question quite difficult. You can help them by looking around their bodies as though you are expecting it to be somewhere in or near them. The more you have explored the resource the easier the client should find this. If they have given any physical sensations as descriptions for the resource, they should find it easier to locate these somewhere; for example: 'And when confidence is warm, whereabouts is that warmth?'.

Bibliography

Sullivan, W. and Rees, J. (2008) *Clean Language: Revealing Metaphors and Opening Minds*, Carmarthen: Crown House Publishing.

8

Hold up a mirror and the client will do the rest

Peter Melrose

Purpose

Clients can sometimes struggle with issues of confidence, especially in the face of tough new challenges. Addressing the underlying issue is one approach, but sometimes clients need only to see themselves clearly in a 'mirror' to find that they know what to do to succeed. New confidence then flows from that realization. The strategy is to hold up the mirror to your client, where the issue is their confidence, not their capability.

Description

In this strategy your role as coach is to enable the client to see a situation more clearly. You will also help the client find the confidence to take the right actions. The key is your belief that the client can do it themselves – with a bit of help from you.

Process

Set some clear objectives: under-confident clients need safety and clear objectives help. Build real trust together to make it okay for them to feel inadequate. Explore the reality around the client and help them fully express their thoughts, feelings and uncertainties. Work from a place of respect but use your own business acumen and organization knowledge to evaluate their take on things. If you see that the issue is indeed confidence, and not capability, focus on holding up the mirror. This is a choice for you to make without sharing that judgement explicitly with the client. It is the mirror's job to do it!

Ask what it would be like if they felt confident to act. What would they do? How would it feel? You might use humour to help them feel more in control by making it all seem very human, not dauntingly 'other'. Do not offer your own ideas or refinements: the process involves working exclusively with your client's resourcefulness. Most importantly, use summarizing statements to bring into sharp relief the choices to act the client would like to make *in their own words*. Offer affirmation and encouragement of the decision to act.

For example, one client was struggling with a predecessor who cast a long shadow. She felt intimidated. I asked what he was doing, what the impact was on her team, how she felt and how she was responding as the team leader. As she talked, I noticed that her desire to take a strong stance in defence of her new role was growing. I asked what she would do and her detailed answer made complete sense. I summarized what she had said and asked her how her words sounded to her. I discovered that it made complete sense to her too! I supported her in her resolve.

The challenge is to help your client identify a 'winning strategy' for themselves. For you, it is also to avoid any distortions in the mirror (for example, a less than winning strategy, unexplored feelings of uncertainty, or your own opinions) and to keep an empathic sense of whether or not the client is indeed finding strength in the process of enquiry.

Pitfalls

These are:

- offering answers and solutions unnecessarily to 'rescue' the client;
- getting impatient with the client's sense of being overwhelmed;

- not keeping a critical eye on the client's sense of things and failing to challenge;
- assuming that your client needs only a mirror when they need more.

9

Moving beyond comfort zones

Caroline Shola Arewa

Purpose

This is a strategy I use with individuals and groups to get people really thinking about where they hold themselves back and how they can elevate levels of confidence and move beyond self-imposed comfort zones.

Description

A comfort zone speaks for itself; it is an area of life where we feel comfortable. In our comfort zone we perform well and feel confident. When we move outside the zone we begin to feel uneasy. Moving outside a comfort zone is frightening by its very nature. People get anxious and fearful when stepping out of the psychological boundaries they have created.

Limiting ourselves in this way prevents us achieving our ultimate performance and success levels. Therefore, it is wise to identify, challenge and expand personal comfort zones.

Process

We all need to expand our comfort zones. What is comfortable will at some point become a limitation. We all had to leave the comfort of the womb in order to grow and develop our potential.

Think of a time when you were forced to move out of your comfort zone, for example when accepting a promotion, parenting teenagers, sitting for meditation or learning to drive on the motorway. When we give in to fear and resistance we can safely excel and give birth to a whole new reality. The ocean in which we feared to swim becomes our new place of sanctuary.

I have devised three steps for expanding comfort zones:

- **Step 1: Identify three of your comfort zones**
  The first step of expanding your comfort zones is to know your limitations. What is holding you back? Are there things you want to do, places you want to go? Yet somehow you speak about it, know the theory, but don't take action. These are your comfort zones. For example, you may lack discipline in your fitness regime, spiritual practice or other areas of your life. You may refuse to let go of your salary to start a business. You know where you are holding back. List three comfort zones.
- **Step 2: Name a comfort zone you are ready to challenge**
  Detail one comfort zone you are ready and willing to change. Break it down, answering the following three questions:

  - How does it hold you back?
  - What are your fears?
  - How do you know you are ready to change?

- **Step 3: Facing the fear and expanding**
  Comfort zones are relative; they are merely the limited perceptions of our minds. Comfort for me is stagnation for another, and my advance is another's retreat. We have nothing to fear in overstepping limiting boundaries we have created. Expansion comes through trust.

  Clearly list the actions you could take to expand your comfort zones. What are you going to do differently in the next seven days?

  Detail specific dates and lifelines and what support you need.

Remember, comfort zones can prevent you achieving your ultimate performance and success levels. Therefore, it is wise to identify, challenge and expand your comfort zones.

You are the author of your life, creating your own destiny.

As the restrictions dissipate, confidence and passion can emerge, propelling you forward.

Pitfalls

There are no known pitfalls!

Bibliography

Arewa, C. S. (2003) *Embracing Purpose, Passion and Peace*, London: Inner Vision Books.

10

Power music

Mags McGeever

Purpose

Music is a very powerful tool. It can evoke very strong feelings – this is especially true for clients with an auditory preference (clients for whom hearing is the main process by which they interpret their version of the world). In particular, music is very effective for encouraging clients. It can significantly increase their motivation and remind them to remain positive and believe in their abilities.

Description

This exercise draws upon the client's frame of reference when it comes to choosing music that has a meaning to the individual.

Process

Ask the client questions to identify their 'power music' or 'power tune'. This will be a different process for each client. Some may be able to tell you instantly, some after you have asked further questions. It might be about situations involving music in which they felt great, concerts they loved, albums they listened to at a time in their life when everything was going really well or lyrics that really speak to them. Others may have to do a bit more investigating.

If a client falls into the last category, you can set them the task between sessions of listening to old albums,

listening to a different radio station, listening more closely
to lyrics – anything that helps them make greater contact
with music. Again, the ideas they come up with themselves
are likely to be the most effective. Ask them to note any
feelings or strong reactions to songs that they have or even
just the songs they've really enjoyed.

Once the client has identified their significant music,
there may be things they can discover about themselves
merely from talking about the feelings associated with it.
Self awareness is a hugely important part of coaching. You
might ask questions such as:

- How do you feel when listening to the music?
- What is it about the music/lyrics that makes you feel that
  way?
- Which feelings would you like to recapture?
- How could you do that?

Alternatively, the music can go into your coach's toolkit
as a resource to employ when greater motivation or self
belief is required for a certain action or goal. It can have a
euphoric effect and give a powerful reminder of the desires
underlying the goal. If the client has not always found time
for completing coaching actions, it may be useful to help
them come up with fun and easy ways of incorporating
the music into their daily schedule. Examples might include
playing it when the alarm goes off in the morning, while
they make their dinner, on their walk to work – but an idea
that the client comes up with themselves would be much
better.

Pitfalls

As mentioned earlier, music is powerful and can evoke very
strong feelings, both positive and negative. The context
within which you are working should tend towards a positive
response but should a certain piece of music bring up difficult feelings for your client, do be prepared to support them
with these.

Bibliography

Blood, A. J. and Zatorre, R. J. (2001). 'Intensely pleasurable responses to music correlate with activity in brain regions implicated in reward and emotion,' *Proceedings of the National Academy of Science*, 98: 11818–11823.
Martin, C. (2001) *Life Coaching Handbook*, Carmarthen: Crown House Publishing.

11

Rescue remedy breathing exercise

Gladeana McMahon

Purpose

The purpose of this exercise is to reduce unwanted emotions in difficult situations.

Description

When facing difficult situations, this breathing exercise provides the client with a strategy that enables them to remain calm by countering the negative biological tendency to produce unhelpful stress hormones such as adrenalin and noradrenalin in stressful situations. These hormones are associated with what has been termed the 'stress response'. When stressed, individuals are likely to experience unhelpful emotions such as anxiety or anger and this breathing exercise helps them manage and gain control over such feelings. It trains the client to breathe in a way that takes the edge off negative feelings and is not noticeable to others. It can therefore be used even when the client is engaged in conversation, for example while they are listening to what the other person is saying.

Process

The client is asked to take in a long, slow breath through his/her nose and then to release it equally slowly through the mouth. While doing so, the client is asked to consciously relax his/her shoulders and to repeat the exercise three or four times.

The coach checks with the client to ascertain whether the individual feels more relaxed when engaging in this exercise. The client is also asked to repeat the exercise as many times as possible, in as many situations as possible, throughout the day. The rationale for practising the exercise is that the more the client practises, the more readily s/he will be able to call upon this relaxation technique when it is needed. If the client does not practice the exercise until it can be called upon easily, the harder it will be to gain the benefits associated with this strategy when the individual actually needs it.

Pitfalls

The coach should check with the client to ensure that s/he does not have any breathing difficulties or suffer from asthma. Although rare, there is a very slim possibility that the exercise could trigger an attack. If the client does suffer from a breathing difficulty, the coach should explain the possibility and the client can decide whether s/he wishes to engage in the strategy.

Bibliography

Davis, M., Eschelman, E. R. and McKay, M. (2000) *Relaxation and Stress Reduction Workbook*, Oakland, CA: New Harbinger Publications.
McMahon, G. (2005) *No More Anxiety: Be your Own Anxiety Coach*, London: Karnac Books.

12

The stand-back strategy

Gladeana McMahon

Purpose

The purpose of this exercise is to provide the client with a strategy for managing unwanted instant emotional reactions.

Description

When facing difficult situations, this strategy enables the client to develop ways of disengaging from unwanted emotions and associated unhelpful behaviours by providing what could be described as a 'circuit breaker', allowing the client to replace the self-defeating emotion and associated behaviour with that of a more self-enhancing nature.

Process

The individual is asked to imagine a situation that has already taken place where s/he experienced an unwanted and self-defeating emotional reaction such as becoming angry. The client then engages in the following process.

The client is asked to go back to the situation s/he has chosen and to remember what actually happened at the time. The coach asks the client to fully engage with the experience by asking the client to describe what s/he was feeling emotionally as well as experiencing physically (for example, how the client's body felt at the time, hot/cold, stomach feeling in knots, etc.).

The coach then asks the client to remember the point

just before s/he acted in a self-defeating manner. When the client is able to do this, the coach asks the client to remember the feelings (physical and emotional) that led up to this point and to think of these as 'early warning signals' that can alert the client in future situations to when s/he is in danger of engaging in unhelpful responses.

The client is then asked to take a slow, deep breath in through their nose and is asked to let it out slowly through the mouth and to count to five in his/her mind on the out-breath, while at the same time visualizing a calming picture or image – this can be any image the client finds calming.

Following this, the client is asked to speak more slowly and provide a statement or comment that would have been more appropriate to deal with the situation.

Once the client has completed the strategy successfully, s/he is asked to undertake this exercise again using two different situations. To ensure that the strategy becomes embedded, the client is asked to undertake the exercise as often as possible as a homework activity.

Pitfalls

This exercise should only be used for those situations where the client's unwanted behaviour is not extreme in nature. To ascertain the severity of unwanted behaviour, the client is asked to rate the degree of emotion experienced on a scale of 0–10 (0 = no emotion and 10 = extreme emotion). If the emotion experienced is rated as 7 or above, this exercise may not be effective as the situation in question may be too challenging for the client at this time. If this is the case, the client is asked to think of a situation where his/her unwanted emotional reaction rates as a 6 or less. If the client can find such situations and can practise this exercise successfully, this will, over time, assist those situations currently rated by the client as 7 or above to become more manageable as the individual will have built up a set of useful coping skills to allow him/her to deal with more challenging situations more effectively.

Bibliography

Bernard, M. E. and Wolfe, J. L. (1993) *The RET Resource Book for Practitioners*, New York, NY: Institute for Rational-Emotive Therapy.

13

The step-up technique

Gladeana McMahon

Purpose

The purpose of this exercise is to help clients identify the cause of concern that may be underpinning a given situation.

Description

The client is asked to imagine what would happen if the situation feared was actively engaged in rather than avoided. By eliciting such information, the client's underlying cause for concern becomes clear. The client is then asked to imagine the worst possible scenario and consider how s/he would cope if such a situation occurred.

Process

The client is asked to close his/her eyes and imagine the situation that s/he fears and, as with other imagery exercises, is asked to fully visualize all factors (that is, sights, sounds, smells, people present, etc.). As the client does so, the coach asks the person to explain what is happening, what thoughts are going through the client's mind and what emotions are being experienced. The coach uses this information to assist the individual to understand what may be at the bottom of the concern being experienced and also to identify the client's worst fear. Once this fear has been identified the coach can assist the client with appropriate strategies to counter such fears.

Pitfalls

The exercise should be abandoned if the client is likely to feel overwhelmed by the emotions s/he experiences.

Bibliography

Lazarus, A. A. (1989) *The Practice of Multimodal Therapy: Systematic, Comprehensive, and Effective Psychotherapy*, New York, NY: Johns Hopkins University Press.

14

Transition to a new level of responsibility

Helen Warner

Purpose

When moving to a more senior level within an organization or a new role, it makes sense to plan ahead in order to make the greatest positive impact when you start. This exercise facilitates such a process.

Description

You've just heard that you've been promoted. The challenges ahead are not clear at this stage and you don't know how you'll meet them, but you know that you want to make a positive impact in your first three months. Here is a quick road map for taking control quickly and effectively during that critical period of transition with strategies based on three years of research into leadership transitions at all levels.

Process

Following these 10 quick strategies will accelerate your learning and ability to add value quickly. It will produce a tailored transition plan for your situation.

- **Promote yourself** – make a mental break from old job to new. Don't assume that what made you a success before will bring you equal success in your new role.
- **Accelerate learning** – understand products, markets, technologies and systems as well as the culture (professional, organizational and geographic) and politics as

soon as possible. Be systematic and focused in achieving this.

- **Match strategy to situation** – identify a clear diagnosis of the situation as this is essential for developing your action plan.
- **Secure early wins** in order to build credibility and create momentum. In the first few weeks, you need to identify opportunities where you can build personal credibility. In the first 90 days, you need to identify ways to create value and improve business results.
- **Negotiate success** – you need to build a productive working relationship with your new boss and manage his/her expectations. It is crucial to gain their support on your 90-day plan.
- **Build your team** – evaluate the team members; do you need to restructure the team to better meet the demands of the situation? Make tough early personnel calls as your capacity to select the right people for the right positions is among the most important drivers of success during your transition.
- **Create a coalition** – as success will depend on your ability to have an influence outside your direct line of responsibility.
- **Identify your key stakeholders** – this will help you further in gaining allies, which will help you to recruit others to increase your resource base and increase the likelihood of achieving your business objectives.
- **Keep your balance** both professionally and personally. Your personal transition is crucial so you will need the right advice-counsel network so that you don't become isolated.
- **Expedite everyone** – help others with their transitions. The quicker you can get your new direct reports up to speed, the more you will help your own performance.

Bibliography

Watkins, M. (2003) *Critical Success Strategies for New Leaders at All Levels: The First 90 Days*, Cambridge, MA: Harvard Business School Press.

15

Unblocking resistance or fear

Joan O'Connor

Purpose

Sometimes coachees want to take a specific action but hold themselves back because of a fear or concern about possible negative consequences. When this happens it can be helpful to take them through the process of thinking about what is the worst thing that can happen and what they would do if it did.

Description

This simple strategy gets a client to imagine the worst scenario and focus on what they would do then. The client typically gains an invaluable insight into a resistance or fear.

Process

Ask the coachee to describe the action they want to take and what they think the worst outcome could be. When they have done this, ask them: 'What would you do then?'. Keep asking them the question until they have identified an action/solution that feels achievable.

Example

Jackie had the opportunity to make changes to her life and career, but was worried that she wouldn't find a job in her preferred choice of work, and that this would leave her financially insecure.

Jackie: What if I don't get another job?
Coach: What would you do then?
Jackie: I'd sell my house and move back to my parents'.
Coach: What would you do then?
Jackie: I'd become an MP.

Jackie was surprised to hear herself say this, and then began to talk about how this had always been something that had interested her, but her working life had got in the way of doing anything about it. Jackie is now working for a different company, in a role that she feels more comfortable with, and with a working schedule that has enabled her to fulfil her duties as a local councillor.

Pitfalls

Some people can become frustrated with or are cynical about being asked the same question repeatedly. It may be necessary to explore their negative response before continuing with this approach.

Bibliography

Neenan, M. and Dryden, W. (2002) *Life Coaching: A Cognitive Behavioural Approach*, Hove: Routledge.

B

Developing as a coach

16

Adding to the data – feelings

Anne Archer

Purpose

This exercise helps the coach to use their own body to gather additional data.

Description

You may have clients who are very good at articulating their problems and issues, who make judgements and rationalize as they talk. You might describe them as being in their head. It is easy to get hooked in to the description and for a while stop being aware of how we are feeling inside – a useful source of additional data.

In this exercise you practise first with a trusted colleague while you develop your awareness of your feelings rather than your thoughts. Choose someone who would also like to develop their ability to hone their own feeling skills; then you can both benefit. You will not be coaching them on any issue and it is important to be clear about this at the start.

Process

It is recommended that you read all the instructions before starting on the process. Find a topic that one of you is going to talk about. Ideally it will be a topic that is playing on their mind a little; however, it should not be anything too overwhelming. It also needs to be something that can be talked about for 10 minutes.

Let's say that your colleague is going to do the talking. Sit down with your chairs next to each other rather than facing. This may feel a bit odd but you do not want to see the person as they speak. The person starts to talk about their topic and all you do is listen. Try and avoid looking at them. As they are talking, notice if there are any sensations in your body and track whether these sensations change during the telling of the story. After 10 minutes, stop and share what you felt and how it changed. Try and stick with a physical description and not an interpretation. So, 'I had a sensation in my upper chest that was restricting' rather than 'I felt anxious when you talked about . . .', or 'You must be anxious'.

It is interesting how often our own sensations are those also described by the other person. The more often you do this exercise the more able you will become to notice your own feelings and to become curious if you pick up any that are unfamiliar.

In phase two of the exercise you start in the same way but then stop the person as you become aware of a feeling. Be tactful and sensitive as you are just testing something out. For example, 'I've just noticed my shoulders are really tight'. The other person may or may not find that they have the same experience. Then continue and interrupt again if something else changes. It is important that you are both aware that this is a practice exercise designed to develop your own awareness as a coach.

In a coaching situation, always include an element of curiosity in your questioning as what you are feeling may not be relevant to them. You might say something like 'I am noticing it's a little hard to catch my breath. I wonder if you are feeling the same?'. If the client says no then move on. All you are doing is offering the possibility and I find these interventions often create a new awareness in the client. Once you develop your own awareness more fully you can use this as a way of helping a coaching client to develop their own ability to notice feelings as they arise.

Pitfalls

You need to ensure that you have a clear contract to deal with a situation where the client becomes distressed, should this arise. The exercise can evoke powerful feelings in both of you; however if set up as an experiment for you both, the learning and benefits to your practice are great.

Bibliography

Joyce, P. and Sills, C. (2001) *Skills in Gestalt Counselling and Psychotherapy*, London: Sage Publications.

17

Bringing yourself into the room: how to use your presence

Julia Cusack

Purpose

The purpose of this exercise is to reveal a potential blind spot, to enhance clients' awareness of their impact on others.

Description

At its simplest, presence means that you as the coach are fully present and totally focused on the client you are working with. You try as far as possible to be in the here and now, bringing all of yourself, and in doing so you allow yourself to be moved by the impact of the client. You then share this with the client as feedback. For many individuals, particularly senior leaders, with whom people have learned not to be direct, this provides a unique combination. The leader is provided with feedback:

- with no hidden agenda, with totally positive intent;
- by someone who experiences their behaviour directly.

The power of this is that it cannot be contradicted, as you are using your own experience.

Process

The process is as follows:

- Notice what you are noticing.
- Play the impact on you back to the coachee.
- Offer it up as feedback.

For example: One client was talking about a meeting he had been invited to by some senior engineers. I noticed that as he was talking, I was becoming anxious, so I played this back to him: 'I notice as you are talking about the meeting, that I am becoming more anxious'. At which point he said 'Yes! You're right, I *am* anxious. I think they've only invited me because they want to show me up, to embarrass me by how little I know about their work'. This led to a fruitful discussion about his assumptions and how true they may be. If he hadn't immediately responded I could have added to the end of my sentence: '. . . and I wonder if that is how you are feeling?'.

Another client cancelled two sessions at short notice, despite our agreement on cancellations, and wasn't available to re-schedule for some considerable time. When I played this back to him I said: 'I notice that you cancelled two sessions and that I found it difficult to get hold of you to re-arrange'. After listening to his answer I enquired: 'I wonder if this is how other people may experience you?'. This prompted a useful discussion around his impact on his team and led to greater insight into his leadership style.

Pitfalls

There is a possibility that you may be rebuffed. Where the truth is hard to hear it may temporarily damage rapport. Be clear and precise with your feedback and restore rapport as soon as you can.

18

Helping your client to learn for themselves, not doing the work yourself

Peter Melrose

Purpose

A client can sometimes fail to see what seems clear to others, including you. The temptation is to save everyone's time by telling the client what you see. However, this more directive approach is not as effective as the strategy of enabling your client to do their own work to learn.

Description

In this strategy you will be helping your client to learn about their situation and find a solution for themselves.

Process

Adopt a strictly non-directive approach in your coaching. Ask open questions; explore the issues without offering your own judgement, solutions or theories. Focus on your client's feelings as well as thoughts. Concentrate on the sense your client is making of things. Be aware of your own emotions in the moment and make them present if there is a resonance with your client, for example 'I'm feeling a sense of frustration as you tell me that your colleagues are refusing to accept your recommendations'. Remember that you do not have to understand the issue, your client does: so, resonant questioning is what is needed, not your analytical ability or insight to solve the client's 'problem'. When you challenge, do so to keep the client fully aware of the contradictions and ambiguities inherent in where they are, for example. 'You tell me you want to do x and that your colleagues are wrong in wanting to do y'. Do not challenge to 'push' your client in any direction, for example, 'So you/they must be right?' or 'Here is another way forward that I can see', but work with your client's energy, for example, 'How do you move forward/feel in this impasse?'

Where there is a 'blind spot' for the client, the organization may have gathered diagnostic data and you may be expected to deliver the message. Resist the pressure to be an advocate. Use this data to enable your client to self reflect, for example 'The data seems to be saying this. What do you make of it?' Help your client explore for themselves what others see without pushing for acceptance on their behalf. You are there to enable your client authentically to engage with the data. The client needs the space to reject all or part of it, if it seems right to them.

New data may be available from recent work experiences to challenge the client's sense of themselves. Retain the focus on how the client can make sense of and resolve the tensions and contradictions. You are there to 'hold your client's feet to the fire', not to fan the flames, nor to put the fire out, nor to press the client to accept the organization's view, nor to allow your client to run away into self deception. The real hard work is for your client who feels the fire burning and has no effective way forward without new learning.

Pitfalls

- Acceptance and change does not happen fast enough for the organization.
- Failing to see the learning taking place because it is not your own 'right answer'.
- Giving in to the client's own desire to 'just tell me'.
- Using this approach when being more direct would be better.

19

Managing and maximizing a relationship with a third party sponsor

Heather Cooper

Purpose

This is a strategy for ensuring that a relationship with a third party sponsor is managed and works well. Clearly, the relationship is important, but can also be complex, for a number of reasons:

- The sponsor is paying for the coaching programme.
- The coaching may link to the relationship with the sponsor.
- The sponsor may also need coaching.
- The coach needs to maintain confidentiality and boundaries.
- The sponsor wants to be kept up to date with progress: they want a return on their investment.
- The sponsor may or may not provide subsequent work for the coach.

These can be conflicting issues and it is worth taking time to define your engagement with each party who is involved in the coaching to ensure clarity on roles, responsibilities and boundaries.

Description

This strategy is designed to help you cover the different aspects of a contract with a third party sponsor. It requires you to be focused and clear about the boundaries and the contract that need to exist for good coaching to take place.

Process

Step 1: At the beginning of a coaching assignment

At the beginning of a coaching assignment, spend time contracting with the different parties:
Contracting with the sponsor:

- Discuss the coaching programme objectives. What are the expectations?
- Find out the organizational context – what does the organization want from the coaching programme?
- Find out how the sponsor will support the coaching programme.
- Decide how to keep up to date without breaking any confidentiality agreement.
- Agree terms and conditions.

Contracting with the coachee:

- Agree the coaching programme objectives.
- Discuss how coaching works and share highlights of any coaching model.
- Agree confidentiality and the boundaries of the coaching.
- Agree terms and conditions.
- Check that the 'chemistry' is good – can you work well together?

Having had these discussions, produce a coaching contract that the coachee and sponsor can approve before the programme starts.

Step 2: During the coaching programme

Once the programme has started and after each coaching session, ask the coachee to discuss their learning with their sponsor. This ensures that:

- the learning from the coaching is being applied back to work;
- the sponsor is reassured about the coachee's progress;
- the coachee can choose what they wish to share, that is, they determine the confidentiality levels.

Periodically liaise with the sponsor part way through the programme. Agree this with the coachee and do a check on the boundaries. Are they happy that the sponsor and coach talk? Are there any no-go areas in the conversation? The update with the sponsor is helpful in providing an understanding on how the coachee is progressing, and therefore helps to frame any coaching interventions.

Step 3: At the end of the coaching programme

Review the progress made, with the coachee and sponsor (both individually and as a trio). This may result in re-contracting for additional sessions or provide closure on the work. It can be very rewarding to complete this evaluation of the work in order to assess what has been achieved and to gain feedback on work as a coach. The review is also crucial for reassuring the value of the coaching programme to the individual and the organization and often leads to the securing of additional work through new assignments.

Pitfalls

There are no known pitfalls to following this clear and objective approach. Failure to adhere, however, is likely to lead to many pitfalls.

Bibliography

McMahon, G. (2005) *Behavioural Contracting, Coach the Coach*, London: Fenman.

20

Managing yourself during the coaching session

Darryl Stevens

Purpose

Remaining psychologically present throughout the entire coaching session is an advanced skill and requires a state of relaxed concentration. Some coaches refer to this as holding the coaching space, achieved through an integrated focus on the client, yourself and the energy between you both. Being able to manage yourself in the moment will help optimize the coaching outcome.

Description

As a professional coach, you bring vast experience to the coaching meeting. While focusing on your client, also focus on yourself and access what is happening for you as the enquiry develops; what happens in the coaching space is often reflective of what happens in similar situations outside of the session. This parallel process can be a powerful observation to share for which you need to recognize your experiences.

Process

Fritz Pearls, the founder of Gestalt therapy, commented that if you are receptive to how someone is, you will learn by seeing it. Access a state of presence before you make contact with your client. I use a Neuro Linguistic Programming (NLP) technique to access a time when I felt totally whole, alert and in flow. A colleague of mine visualizes himself holding the client in cupped hands using a psychosynthesis approach. Other coaches refer to this preparation as finding their centre.

During the session, use your body as a tuning fork and recognize any areas of tension, how you are breathing and moving, for example. Also check in with your thoughts and ask yourself how you are finding the session: is it fast paced, are you bored or finding it hard to stay with the discussion, is your mind racing ahead? Once you have accessed this information, ask yourself, 'What is this telling me and what should I do with it?'. This may result in an implicit or explicit action. Timing is important, as is the manner in which you apply the information, ensuring that it is appropriately tailored to the client and the nature of the session.

After each session, take time to reflect by drawing a time line and recalling what happened for you during the meeting. Note the points of self-management and the choices you made, along with any thoughts on what you may have done differently. This exercise will enhance your ability to blend the self-management techniques into your coaching.

Pitfalls

Be sure to contract with the client that they agree to you using self-management techniques, also remembering that you are there for the client's agenda and self-management choices should be to the benefit of the coachee. Look out for signs of transference and counter-transference – absorbing the client's emotions and energy, which in turn dominate your behaviour. And finally, while managing yourself, you may miss something from your client. This will be less apparent as self-management techniques become part of your coaching approach.

21

Pre-coaching ritual

Mags McGeever

Purpose

The purpose of this strategy is to help you become clear and focused on your client prior to a coaching session.

Description

For some, a pre-coaching ritual may enhance listening ability and presence in a coaching session. In addition to your practical preparation (such as going over any notes, switching off your phone and ensuring you have all the necessary stationery, etc.), mental preparation is very important. It allows you, as a coach, to put aside your own 'stuff', feel calm and focused and be able to listen one hundred percent to the client. A personalized ritual that you perform before every session may be a good way of achieving this.

Process

This is not for use during a session but in advance of the session as part of your preparation:

- Think of an action or process which you enjoy that is likely to make you feel calm, energized or any other quality you want to enhance. Some suggestions: visualization, sitting quietly with a hot drink, writing a list of the things on your mind and then placing it in a drawer and closing it, a yoga posture, a mantra, a short meditation, dancing madly to your favourite song or a symbolic gesture such as pouring your thoughts down the sink. As is the case with your clients, the most powerful ritual will be the one you come up with yourself.

- Repetition of your personal ritual is likely to increase its power. As your mind starts to recognize that this action means it is time for coaching, it will automatically begin to prepare.
- Try to find a way to incorporate this ritual into your coaching schedule that means you will always have time to do it and it will not be squeezed out by other events.

Pitfalls

This exercise may not be so effective at first until you become skilled at de-cluttering your mind as a matter of course. Persistence, however, will reap massive benefits.

Bibliography

O'Connor, J. and Seymour, J. (2003) *Introducing NLP Neuro-Linguistic Programming*, London: Thorsons.

22

Redefining the meaning of feedback and creating a unique feedback pattern

Elspeth Campbell

Purpose

The purpose of this strategy is to develop a meaningful feedback process that enables the stakeholders to determine the success of the coaching.

Description

During the contracting phase for a piece of coaching, we aim to develop a feedback pattern that requires the client to evaluate the coaching with their stakeholders, including their line manager. The line manager takes responsibility to feed back to the coach useful effects of coaching. This has a dual purpose:

- confidentiality – a safe coaching space can be created for the client to discover, become vulnerable, experiment;
- it prepares fertile ground for growth in the client as their stakeholders notice the effects of coaching.

Process

1 Brief the sponsor commissioning the coaching about this approach at project inception, covering the points above. This key discussion is crucial in establishing a shared understanding of how the potential power of coaching can be realised with helpful structures in place. Possible constraints to a mutual understanding are:

- if the sponsor's approach requires that the coach is chosen through a chemistry meeting, the sponsor may resist having this discussion beforehand;
- if the sponsor's primary purpose is to discover more about the coachee's performance from the coach, the coaching effectively becomes construed as a replacement for line managing the individual.

It could be that at this initial phase of contracting it is discovered that the sponsor's and the coach's approach to coaching differ too greatly, so it may become necessary for the coach to decline the project.

2 Discuss confidentiality during the initial meeting so that the client understands how the feedback process ensures confidentiality and learning transfer. It is useful here to start with exploring how the coachee would view a breach of confidentiality.

3 Run part of the second coaching session as a contracting meeting, including the line manager, and other sponsor if appropriate, where the feedback process is explored. The contracting meeting needs careful planning so that both the coachee and the line manager can express themselves in constructive ways that pave the way for useful conversations in future. It is advisable to discuss this with the line manager beforehand so that s/he has an idea of what is expected of her/him.

4 Encourage the coachee to make contact with people in the organization to ensure confidentiality. Where this is not appropriate, communication with the organization is done with the coachee's permission and the coachee is copied in to the communication.

5 Only feed back to the sponsor impressions of the organization, themes of patterns emerging, etc., once the client's contract has been completed.

Pitfalls

A possible pitfall is the sponsor's eagerness to know of the coach's impressions of the organization. These can be given without specific reference to the coachee. The sponsor sometimes needs some reassurance and so it's helpful to keep in good contact.

Bibliography

Leimon, A., Moscovici, F. and McMahon, G. (2005) *Essential Business Coaching*, Hove: Brunner-Routledge.

23

Rusty or out of practice
Julia Cusack

Purpose

As a budding or even as an established coach, there may be periods in your coaching career where you do little or no coaching. Perhaps your business has been taking you in a different direction and you're spending your time on other activities; maybe you are beginning to build a client base; or the opportunities to coach have been sporadic. Similar to the woodcutter in Stephen Covey's *Seven Habits of Highly Effective People* (whose tool had become less effective), you too may need to sharpen your saw. To refresh your best authentic coaching self, here are activities you can pursue.

Description

Reflecting

1 Browse through previous coaching session reflection notes and pick out one or two that were particularly significant to you. Note down in your learning journal how you have incorporated those experiences and learning subsequently.
2 Read through your learning journal from an earlier period, for example a year ago or where you remember a significant learning experience. Write down how you might tackle this type of coaching situation differently today. If you would tackle it in the same way, also note down the reasons why you would do so. This can really

help you build your confidence in how far you have come and your ability to keep learning.

Doing

1 By agreement with a colleague (preferably another coach), take a conversation you were going to have anyway and explicitly use it as a mini-practice session. Ask for the other person's feedback afterwards and make reflection notes as you would for a normal coaching session.
2 Find an opportunity to observe fellow coaches or coaches-in-training, perhaps as a facilitator on a course. If possible, arrange to provide them with feedback on their coaching practice, which will sharpen your observation and feedback skills.
3 Speak to your supervisor, or if you don't have one, given that you are feeling rusty, find a colleague or fellow coach who knows your style or has seen you coach and ask for feedback on what they really appreciate about your coaching style and/or approach.

Reading

1 Pick a coaching book you have enjoyed and/or one that has been recommended, which gives plenty of examples of excerpts of coaching interventions. These practical tips and examples will help refresh your knowledge and raise your awareness of tools and techniques you may have forgotten. Make a note of the key ones.
2 Go through this book and pick out two or three strategies you would like to try out. Find a willing volunteer, or try them out on yourself.

Process

1 Either during the 'down' time between coaching assignments or directly in advance of your next coaching session, select at least one activity from each section in this book, list them and plan when you will do them.
2 Record your results in your learning journal or diary.

Committing your activities to paper is a key part of the process.

Pitfalls

Not recognizing the need to undertake the exercise.

Bibliography

Covey, S. R. (2004) *The Seven Habits of Highly Effective People*, New York, NY: Simon & Schuster.

24

Sometimes coping is as good as it gets

Peter Melrose

Purpose

Coaches usually feel a desire to help clients improve their personal effectiveness. Sometimes circumstances make it very hard for the client to do more than survive through a crisis. This strategy is about recognizing when to adjust away from improvement goals and help your client just cope.

Description

Sometimes a client can be in a difficult situation with no obvious way forward. This strategy helps the client to stay with the current challenges and at the same time to become more resourceful.

Process

First, help your client explore the business context and the degree of pressure they face. Explore how they see the personal challenge of change and improvement. Though change does not come without pain, the risk sometimes is that pressure and pain will overwhelm the client. The challenge is to recognize what support the client most needs in the moment. Explore this openly with the client. Then agree coaching objectives.

While exploring these objectives, keep your senses fully open throughout the coaching process to your client's experience of pressure and their personal resilience. Events might take a sudden turn for the worse, or the client's resilience might rapidly erode. Some clients will readily display the pain and emotion they feel in the safety of the coaching conversation. Many others find it very hard to do so as it can feel like personal weakness.

Your challenge is emotionally to resonate with your client to engage with the impact of the pressure they feel and to explore whether coping is the most effective immediate strategy for them. This is the moment to help your client recognize whether or not their needs from coaching have changed: personal improvement may have to take a lesser priority.

For example, one client was struggling to lead his team effectively and dealing with an unpredictable and aggressive boss. He wanted to address how his drive, intellectual confidence (but weakening self-confidence) and lack of 'feel' for the organization culture were getting in his way. But soon the relationship reached a breaking point. When I explored his feelings about it, his greatly increased upset and pain were very clear in the safety of the coaching relationship. I learned that in the organization he was behaving defiantly and aggressively. He recognized that this 'default' behaviour would make things worse and agreed that personal survival was now uppermost in his mind. We agreed that, though there was still much for him to learn about his personal effectiveness, continuing to focus on perceived leadership flaws would risk adding to his stress, and get in the way of a personal strategy of thoughtful coping.

In such circumstances, agree new objectives with your client and use the process to help them fully to accept the reality of the pressure they face, to create reflection time to manage emotional distress and to plan how to operate effectively at work to minimize further damage. In other words, to live with the reality of the pain, but finding resilience in thoughtful coping.

Pitfalls

- Not letting go enough of the performance improvement agenda.
- Over or underestimating the impact of pressure on your client.
- Not allowing enough space for pain to be safely expressed.

25

Three-part breathing exercise

Caroline Shola Arewa

Purpose

This exercise can be used to create a focus for yourself before and after coaching sessions. It can also be used with clients to help them relax and focus at the beginning of a session. It can be used successfully in tele-coaching sessions.

Description

A timeless technique that can be used to calm the mind, create clarity and reduce stress and anxiety. I detail the exercise in three easy steps.

Process

This exercise is best done sitting comfortably in a chair with your spine upright. Let your feet be flat on the floor about 18 inches apart. Place your hands on your knees, your palms facing upwards. Draw your chin slightly towards your chest in order to lengthen the back of your neck. Relax your shoulders and allow yourself to feel open across your chest. Close your eyes and open your mouth. Let your face soften. Have an expansive sense of taking up as much space in your body as you can. Let go of any tightness or tension. Release and relax your whole body. This preparation need only take a few seconds.

Now give attention to your breath. Place one hand over your lower abdomen.

- **First part**
  Breathe in through your nose *slowly and fully*, raising your abdomen. Open your chest and completely fill your lungs (your hand should lift upwards).
- **Second part**
  Hold your breath comfortably, keeping your body totally still for a count of four. (This can be increased with practice.)
- **Third part**
  Exhale slowly through your nose and empty your lungs completely. Feel your abdomen pulling down towards your spine (your hand will be lowered).

Repeat this three-part breath three to seven times. Let your body relax and your mind become clear. Continue to focus on your breath. This exercise can be done for two minutes, five minutes, 10 minutes or more depending on the time available and your level of concentration.

This exercise allows full and correct use of the breathing apparatus. It restores movement to the diaphragm and intercostal muscles. Five times more oxygen is taken into the lungs and transported around your body's cells. This helps to flush out toxins. The nervous system relaxes and concentration improves. The mind begins to slow its activity and become clearer. An ability to control the breath is fundamental to reducing stress, enhancing health and maximizing success.

Pitfalls

The only word of caution relates to the short retention of breath in the second part of the breathing exercise. If this feels uncomfortable at all, the exercise can be done using only the first and third parts. The count of four as outlined above is a suitable starting place for healthy individuals.

Bibliography

Arewa, C. S. (2003) *Embracing Purpose, Passion and Peace*, London: Inner Vision Books.

C

Developing specific skills and strategies

26

Attitude awareness – impact and influencing

Gill Hicks

Purpose

The purpose of this approach is to help a client adopt a helpful attitude when seeking a promotion.

Description

In order to succeed in business today, it is just as essential for business professionals to display appropriate attitudes as it is for them to be good academically. This is often referred to as having a high level of EQ (emotional intelligence). Attitudes are displayed by behaviour, appearance, body language and voice. The following is a good exercise for business individuals who are seeking promotion or are seeking to raise their level of impact internally or externally.

Process

First, ask the client to assume a 'third position' – to stand in the shoes of a client or senior manager and ask them which attitudes they would be looking for from a successful individual in the role of 'X' (in the case of a client seeking promotion, the role would be the one they are aspiring to). Push the client until they come up with at least 10 winning attitudes but ideally more. A few examples might be:

- positive
- energized

- creative
- enthusiastic
- leadership qualities
- dependable
- business focused
- ability to deal with stress
- team player
- trustworthy
- solution focused
- professional.

Ask the client to describe what they would see and hear to know that an individual had the above qualities.

Next, ask the client to assess themselves against each quality. Do others experience this attitude of your client all the time, some of the time or rarely? How would others *know* that your client has these winning attitudes? What are the development areas, what could your client do differently?

Example

My client Christopher was due to start with a new company as a sales manager. Prior to starting his employment he was invited to attend an offsite Team Building Day and was concerned as to the impression he would make. He was carrying 'baggage' from his old firm where he had been told a year earlier by the sales director that he was not thought capable of 'ever' being promoted. After completing the above exercise along with one or two other interventions, Christopher went to the Team Building Day feeling very confident and made a very powerful impression. He was told he had fitted into the team exceptionally well – indeed an outside facilitator on the day was asked to guess who the new candidate was and he could not guess that it was Christopher.

Pitfalls

Ensure that the client comes up with attitude words – if their attitudes are poor and they believe they are good at their job, they will have a tendency to concentrate on deliverables.

Also ensure that your client is in third position before they describe the winning attitudes and that they feel sufficiently safe to give an honest appraisal of their strengths and development points.

Bibliography

Knight, C. and Glaser, J. (2007) *Create Image with Type, Image and Color*, Hove: RotoVision.

27

Building a high performing team

Helen Warner

Purpose

This is a simple strategy to help individuals or groups of people think about how they operate as part of a team or manage a team.

Description

You don't have to be Alex Ferguson to have the skills to build and lead a high performing team. However, if you have a team of individuals rather than a group united in their goals and values, you may not be leveraging on the full potential of the team you have.

Process

Using the diagram in Figure 2, ask the individual or group to think about each 'spoke' for the team and/or for individuals within the team using a traffic light system: green for 'effective', amber for 'potential for improvement' and red for 'area of concern'. This will help identify barriers to creating a fully effective group and coaching can be focused on an action plan to achieve a positive outcome.

Pitfalls

None.

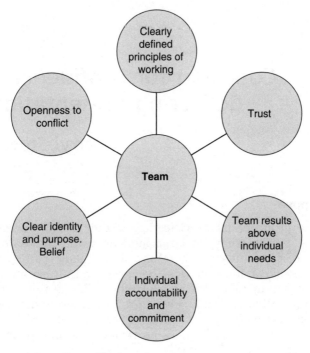

Figure 2 Dimensions of high performance

Bibliography

Adapted from Blanchard, H. K., Carew, D. and Parisi-Carew, E. (2000) *The One Minute Manager Builds High Performance Teams*, New York, NY: HarperCollins.

28

Coaching for confidence in delivering presentations

Darryl Stevens

Purpose

Ask a group of business leaders if they look forward to giving presentations to large audiences and the majority will respond negatively. Many individuals panic, feel self-conscious, have physical reactions and ultimately lack confidence in this area of leadership. This is linked to a concept called 'self-talk', also known as 'internal dialogue'. This is derived from Tim Gallwey's studies and publications on 'The Inner Game' where he reviews the impact of the mindset upon performance.

Description

There are several good approaches to addressing negative self-talk, with a blend of cognitive behavioural therapy (CBT), positive psychology and neuro linguistic programming (NLP) working well in achieving sustainable shift. The approach is based on reframing existing negative thoughts into positive ones and focuses on addressing the components of Kant's paradigm of see → think → feel → do (see Peltier, 2001).

Process

Start with an enquiring dialogue into what the client goes through before, during and after the presentation. The power of playing inner-thoughts on a loud speaker, that is, making the implicit explicit, can often be revealing in itself.

I had a senior client talk for the first time about her brothers laughing at her when on stage as a child. Another became emotional when he recalled how a previous manager constantly criticized his ability to speak in front of a group. These anchored experiences were inhibiting their presentation performance and pointed to the cause of the respective pre-presentation and on-stage anxiety.

Having identified where the negative self-talk is at its greatest, take the client back to their last presentation and start to relive it. On a piece of paper (see Figure 3), invite the client to capture on the left of the page the negative thoughts that were experienced at this time. Below that, ask them to state how they felt and behaved as a result of this self-talk. Once these current thoughts, feelings and actions have been captured, shift and positively reframe them into ones they would like to experience. Ask the client for their desired reactions and emotional approach, using the bottom right hand space to record their answers. Moving upwards on the

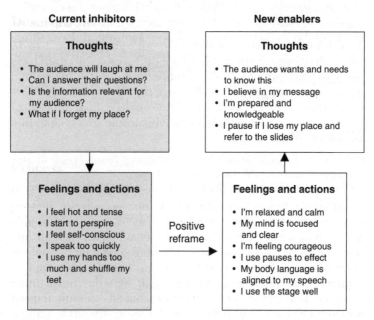

Current inhibitors

Thoughts
- The audience will laugh at me
- Can I answer their questions?
- Is the information relevant for my audience?
- What if I forget my place?

Feelings and actions
- I feel hot and tense
- I start to perspire
- I feel self-conscious
- I speak too quickly
- I use my hands too much and shuffle my feet

New enablers

Thoughts
- The audience wants and needs to know this
- I believe in my message
- I'm prepared and knowledgeable
- I pause if I lose my place and refer to the slides

Feelings and actions
- I'm relaxed and calm
- My mind is focused and clear
- I'm feeling courageous
- I use pauses to effect
- My body language is aligned to my speech
- I use the stage well

Positive reframe

Figure 3 **Reframing for presentation confidence**

paper, now ask your client what their new self-talk should be to invoke the new feelings and actions described. It is important to use the present tense when reframing so that the desired outcome is experienced 'now'.

Having completed the exercise, ask your client to visualize the next speaker opportunity using the new enablers identified. Ask them to state what they now see, think, feel and what they are now doing in the presentation. Ask them to talk it aloud to re-enforce their new self-talk. You can also incorporate an NLP anchor point, inviting your client to squeeze their thumb and forefinger together, for example, as a signal attached to the new positive cognitions and emotions. This can be used to recall the reframed state at the next presentation.

Pitfalls

A lack of confidence in giving presentations may be related to a past experience. If this is revealed during the coaching session, be mindful as to how you address it and be aware of the boundaries between therapy, counselling and coaching. While deep exploration can be powerful in creating sustainable change for your client, to remain within the sphere of coaching, any historic content should be used to identify what impact it has for the client in the present.

Bibliography

Gallwey, W. T. (1975, 1986) *The Inner Game of Tennis*, London: Pan Books in association with Jonathan Cape.
Peltier, B. (2001) *Psychology of Executive Coaching*, London: Routledge.

29

Confidence building with body language

Gill Hicks

Purpose

The purpose of this strategy is to make a client aware of their body language.

Description

It is interesting that the mind, body and voice all work as one complete unit, which means that if we change one of these factors, the others cannot help but change also. This strategy is demanding of you as a coach as you must be very aware of your own body language. You will be demonstrating to the client their gestures, stance, posture and movement.

Process

Exercise 1

First, assume a 'confident posture' yourself. If sitting, ensure that your body, legs and head are facing the client. Both feet should be firmly on the floor in a 'grounded' position (or if your legs are crossed at least one foot should be firmly on the floor). If standing, your feet should be slightly apart, with weight evenly distributed. Imagine a thread pulling you up from the back of your head to be as tall as you can, giving you a straight spine. Your torso should be very slightly inclined towards your client. Your shoulders should be down and back; feel your shoulders getting wider – 'taking up space'. Your arms and hands should be uncrossed and open. Your head should be upright with your chin parallel to the floor. *Smile*. Ask the client what they would assume about your level of confidence (and notice your own feelings).

Next, demonstrate what you see your client doing. You might slightly exaggerate and tell them you are exaggerating their gestures (you don't want to knock their confidence further!). Look out for a curved spine, a torso leaning back, a chin lowered, arms that cover the body, a part of their body (feet, legs, face, torso) not directly pointing towards you. As before, ask them what they would feel about your level of confidence – and notice your own feelings.

Direct them to assume the confident body language as detailed above. You should see a big difference; give them appropriate encouragement. It is particularly helpful if you have a mirror or video recording equipment to hand, allowing the client to see the differences you have seen. Ask them how they feel.

If your client has ever studied martial arts, the 'confident posture' will be familiar to them and they will remember it as the 'xyz stance'. Your client will need to practise regularly so you might need to ask them where, when and what will remind them to do this.

Exercise 2

Watch your client walking both towards and away from you. To raise both the appearance and feeling of confidence, encourage them to walk with the confident posture (above), without rushing and with a slight swing to the arm(s). Weight should be quite centred, creating an effect of a 'glide'. Ask them how they feel and feed back what you see.

Example

Janet was due to start a new job, having had two years at home with her baby. She had been in her previous position for several years and was terrified of meeting new people. She was also terrified of travelling into London, being surrounded by 'all those strangers looking at her'. She admitted that she had hated the travel to and from work in the last job for the same reason. Janet agreed to leave our office with the 'new walk', including looking at the people around rather than looking at the pavement. Six months after our coaching finished, Janet emailed me and said that her 'life was changed'. Now, she always walks with a swing in her arm, looks at people around her – and she loves her job.

Pitfalls

- Check out your own natural body language with a mirror first, ensuring that it is consistently confident before advising others.
- When asking the client how they feel in the confident position, they may say that it feels strange or even uncomfortable. That is fine. Holding the body differently does feel strange, but with lots of practice it will feel very empowering. The key is for them to see what a difference it makes, so if a mirror is not available at the coaching session, get their commitment to checking it out at home.

Bibliography

Kuhnke, E. (2007) *Body Language for Dummies*, Hoboken, NJ: John Wiley & Sons.

30

Creating an impact at work – appearance

Gill Hicks

Purpose

This exercise aims to make it clear to a client how their appearance can have an impact on an outcome.

Description

If your client is seeking promotion at work and feels they are doing a great job, but that their talent is not being recognized, ask yourself whether your client looks the part of the new role. It is a strange phenomenon that people who look like they will get on in an organization are often the ones promoted, but they are not necessarily any more able than those who are passed over! It may seem grossly unfair, but it is a fact of life that many of us are greatly influenced by what we take in visually – as the packaging industry knows only too well!

Those of us who are at all visually influenced regularly make some massive assumptions about people and their state of mind from their appearance. Just think of comments like 'You look very smart today – are you off for an interview?'. Or you look around the office and feel somebody is unlikely to rise through the ranks much beyond their current position.

Process

Let's imagine that your client is aspiring to the role of financial director (FD). Ask them to imagine a conference room full of FDs. In the room there are one or two who stand out as looking particularly successful. Ask your client to describe *in precise detail* what these people look like. If your client is female, she should imagine a room full of female FDs, and if male, then male FDs. Prompt your client. For example, ask them what their hair is like – modern, conservative, on or off the face, well styled or not, recently trimmed, etc. Go through every item visible – suit, shirt or top, tie or jewellery, make-up, socks/stockings, bag and shoes. Prompt on quality, fit, level of maintenance, textures, colour and appropriateness of each item for the workplace and the culture they work in. Write down the 'recipe' for your client. Ask your client to imagine that they are working in the costume department of a film production company and ask what they would change for the audience to be able to distinguish between the more senior FD and the less senior financial controller.

The absolute key to creating a successful professional impact through appearance at work is *consistency* and *a high level of maintenance*. Wearing a smart suit for the important meeting and just a shirt and crumpled trousers for the rest of the week becomes 'play acting'.

If you can see that your client doesn't 'look the part' and you feel they need a little more professional help than you are able to offer, do suggest that they consider seeing a professional image consultant/coach. However, image consultants, like any profession, do vary enormously in their experience and expertise so do suggest that your clients ask about experience and training. A national and international list of highly trained consultants can be found at www.houseofcolour.co.uk. Also ask if the sponsoring company is willing to pay – it is a relatively small investment for developing and retaining talent.

Example

Jeremy is an IT team leader and we had a number of objectives to cover, including confidence building, assertiveness and management skills. At our second meeting, he was wearing a short-sleeved open-neck shirt – as before, yet walking round his department I noticed a number of people in suits and nobody else wearing short sleeves. The company agreed to finance a day on image and we found the colours, styles, textures, etc. that gave Jeremy a greater appearance of authority. His first investment was several long-sleeved shirts and a few ties, which he has worn consistently. The change of image has contributed towards Jeremy's assessment of his confidence going from 20 per cent to 80 per cent over a six-month period and he is now being groomed for promotion.

Pitfalls

Sometimes people link their appearance to who they think they are. A coach can help them to see the impact their appearance has without it appearing as personal criticism.

Bibliography

Everett, L. (2004) *Walking Tall: Key Steps to Total Image Impact*, London: Lesley Everett.

31

Decisions by intuition

Mags McGeever

Purpose

The purpose of this exercise is to help a client make decisions using their intuition.

Description

Some clients have difficulty making decisions. A useful but often under-used tool here is intuition. Often, a person does know deep down what is best for them. Consider the old example of tossing a coin. If it comes down heads and you notice yourself disappointed with the result you know to go with the other option. The strategy presented here is a slightly expanded version of the same principle, which has the advantage of allowing the client to feel that a situation has been more fully reasoned and thought through. As authors such as Malcolm Gladwell (2000) have suggested, this thinking is probably not necessary. Your brain can make the right decision for you in an instant. However, it can be reassuring for some to consider something more fully. You may use this strategy to help clients increase their confidence in their decision-making ability.

Process

1 Guide the client through separate visualizations for each option open to them. Ideally, visualizations will not be too close in time. Perhaps the client will do one or more of them alone outside of the session.

2 If the client is going to do the visualization outside of the session, you may assist them by giving a print-out of the visualization wording or even recording an audio version for them.
3 For each option, ask the client to visualize the situation were they to take that course of action. What would they say? Do? See? Hear? Where would it take place? When? What would they wear? If another person is involved, what would they say? Do? Etc. Help them to make the visualization as detailed and vivid as possible.
4 Once you have done this, ask the client to notice how they feel.
5 Your client may wish to note down or draw any words, picture, emotions that come to mind. On the other hand, they may not. Often intuition cannot be put into words.
6 Repeat this process for each of the options the client is considering.
7 Once all options have been visualized and the feelings relating to those visualizations noted, it is often startlingly clear which choice the client wants to make.
8 The effectiveness of this exercise may be strengthened by the client putting their hand on their heart or stomach during the visualization process.

Pitfalls

Everyone has a different way in which they prefer to make decisions and for some they may simply not be happy with this exercise as it does not appear to have sufficient logic. As with all exercises, you want it to be useful for the client. If it does not work for them, simply encourage them to make confident decisions in a way that is more suitable for their thinking style.

Bibliography

Gladwell, M. (2002) *The Tipping Point*, New York, NY: Back Bay Books.
Spence, R. (2006) *Information Visualization: Design for Interaction*, London: Prentice Hall.

32

Enriching a leader's influence style through a deepening understanding of their impact on others

Elspeth Campbell

Purpose

The purpose of this exercise is to enable the client to become more effective at influencing others.

Description

I use influence styles questionnaires LSI 1&2 from Human Synergistics (HS/UK Ltd: www.humansynergistics.co.uk), which involves a 360-degree feedback process. Their use is particularly enlightening with senior managers where a change in behaviour in the manager has resulted in having less influence than is necessary for the role, or has had an adverse influence on their relationships and therefore on their ability to achieve. The 12 styles are: Humanistic – encouraging, Affiliative, Approval, Conventional, Dependent, Avoidance, Oppositional, Power, Competitive, Perfectionistic, Achievement and Self-Actualizing.

Process

This influence styles tool is used in the following way:

- **Choice making:** If, during the first coaching meeting, influence styles appear to be an issue that will fall within the remit of the coaching contract, I discuss with the manager the option of using this process and what it entails, and send a sample report, so that s/he can make an active choice. Choice making is an indicator of the manager's sense of agency (Oliver, 2005) and gives me a glimpse of some core inner resilience that will enable him/her to learn from this powerful process rather than be threatened by it. The decision to use the process will shape my proposal for the length and intensity of the coaching contract, as it is time consuming and influence behaviours take time to change. A contract of at least eight sessions over six months is appropriate. The manager's choice to go ahead would become part of coaching session 2, which includes the logistics of when to do it, who s/he will use as 5–10 respondents, how these people will be invited to participate and anticipating their response to being invited, the manager's expectations and concerns. Giving attention to what is being created within the relational dynamics by the choice to use this tool is apt because this is what influence is about. Those chosen as respondents could become allies in the manager's quest to change behaviour during the course of the coaching contract.

- **LSI 1:** The manager completes this questionnaire about his/her own styles of influence, returns it to Human Synergistics for computer scoring and then it comes to me for interpreting.
- **LSI 1 discussion:** The profile report produced enables the manager's reflection on attitudes, thought processes and influence intention as facilitated by the coaching conversation. It involves how their predominantly used influence styles, or least used, show in their behaviour and how these may be helping or hindering what the manager wants to do, and what the organization requires that s/he does. Also discussed are departmental and organizational cultural norms about 'what is expected around here' and how aspects of the manager's style of influence complement, contrast or collude with this. Another topic is anticipating how the respondents may respond. There is a LSI 1 workbook to take away and some work for

the manager to do by observing him/herself in action to gather experiences of their influence before the next coaching session.

- **Inviting 5–10 respondents:** The manager chooses respondents who represent significant stakeholders in his/her performance and ability to influence: line manager, staff, internal customer, colleague within peer group, family member. The following criteria assist the choice: respondents who know the manager well enough to comment meaningfully, are interested, have time to respond, some being supporters of the manager and some not so. Respondents answer the questionnaire confidentially and return it direct to me.
- **LSI 2 discussion:** An aggregate profile of the responses is produced and enables the manager to learn the impact of his/her behaviour on these people. The coaching conversation assists discovery of congruencies and discrepancies between how the self is perceived and how others experience the manager, and the importance of this. Learning occurs about which influence style to use on different occasions, given the context, and about how to be adaptable and to make wise choices around this. Practicing variations on current influence style continues throughout the remainder of the coaching contract.

Pitfalls

As with all such interventions, it requires positioning with the client and the coach needs to be able to explain the process to those who may be sceptical.

Bibliography

Oliver, C. (2005) *Reflexive Inquiry*, London: Karnac Books.

33

Handling poor performance/ unacceptable behaviour

Penny Swinburne

Purpose

Addressing issues of poor performance or unacceptable behaviour is a much needed but often avoided part of managerial competence, so clients are very grateful for this tool. DESC, borrowed from assertiveness training, is for planning how to raise these issues. It can be useful for new managers, through to senior managers for whom interpersonal skills were less important earlier in their careers. It can be used flexibly, from stopping poor performance early on to a serious pre-discipline situation and with colleagues, subordinates and others in raising other difficult issues. The variation is in the delivery; the DESC planning remains the same.

Description

The exercise simply works through planning the four stages of DESC, as described below. The exercise brings clarity about the issue to be raised and builds confidence in raising it. Planning can be followed by practising the delivery.

Process

1 Outline DESC, using an example, for example a subordinate being late.

- **D** escribe the behaviour – what they are doing, not what they are. (*I've noticed that you've been late arriving on several occasions lately.*)

- **E** xplain the effects – on you/other relevant people, including feelings if useful. *(This means that opening the post has had to be done by your colleagues, putting their work back and it's beginning to cause bad feelings in the team.)*
- **S** tate what you need them to change. (*I really need you to be getting in on tim*e.)
- **C** onsequences for them: good if the behaviour does change *(And then you will be able to do the post as you should and team feelings will be restored.)*; bad if the behaviour does not change (*I will have to move to a formal warning if it continues.*)

2 Work through DESC with your client, using their situation. Points to be clear on:

- **D** is best expressed in 'I' form.
- The **S** needs to tie in with the **D**. The behaviour you are addressing does not change halfway through. Clarity is key, as they will only have the receiver's attention for a short time.
- **C** is planned to give confidence that it is worth raising the issue. For example, if it is inconsequential (I, the manager, will feel better!), it's not worth raising it.

3 Coaching on what to say and how to say it:

- Using an 'adult-to-adult' style/non-verbal behaviour.
- Where to stop to effectively move the situation forward: for example, often after the **D** and **E**, then seek reactions (*I'm wondering what's changed to suddenly make this happen*). Sometimes just raising the **D** is enough for the person to realise that they have to change.
- How hard to push for change: for example, if the situation has been raised several times, it becomes appropriate to include **C** straight away and/or to use the technique of 'action replay' to repeat the required change in **S**.

Role playing the scenario with feedback can help the client check out delivery, particularly clarity, adult-to-adult interpersonal style and how the conversation may go forward.

Pitfalls

None. There are no guarantees, but it increases the likelihood of success significantly.

Bibliography

Bower, S. A. and Bower, G. H. (2004) *Asserting Yourself: A Practical Guide for Positive Change*, Jackson, TN: Perseus.

34

Impact – voice

Gill Hicks

Purpose

This purpose of this exercise is to enable the client to improve the impact their voice has on others.

Description

The voice has a huge impact on others when we communicate verbally. We can make a phrase such as 'I am really enthusiastic about this project' sound genuine, confident, sarcastic, uncertain or plain unenthusiastic! Think of the voice like a musical instrument with a wide range of notes, yet many people just play the 'middle C' and if the middle C for your client is bored, uncertain or bullying, they are unlikely to make a positive impact on others, no matter how hard they work. The strange thing about the voice is that most of us would prefer to bury our head in the sand and do anything to avoid hearing our voice recorded to assess how it sounds! You do not have to be a fully trained voice coach to use this exercise, though it is a good idea to try it out yourself before working with a client.

Process

Using a hand-held voice recorder, ask your client to tell you something about business, or get them to read a short passage from the newspaper. Play it back to them and ask them to assess it out of 10 for the following qualities:

- enthusiasm;
- energy;
- confidence;
- authority;
- approachability;
- boredom;
- uncertainty.

The key to an interesting voice is a full breath and clear articulation. If your client's voice sounds quiet, uncertain and/or bored, suggest that they practise standing tall, fully exhale and take a deep abdominal breath without the shoulders rising. If they find this difficult, they should practice daily between sessions.

If the words are not particularly clear and there is little range in the client's voice, suggest that they say: 'Peter Piper picked a peck of pickled pepper corns', but over-articulating, that is over-emphasizing, the lip movements (you demonstrate first and you should both be in stitches!). Record them during this exercise and then play back it back.

Ask the client to re-record the passage, working on their weaker areas, inviting them to talk in what to them would sound extreme and 'silly' tones. Playing the recording back, they are likely to be very surprised that 'extreme' approachability (say, talking as they would to a young child), far from sounding silly, does in fact sound highly approachable. The client should purchase their own voice recorder and practice daily, stretching themselves to a point that it does sound overdone on the playback, at which point they will know to revert a notch or two.

My client Audrey was frustrated that she had not received what she felt to be the promotion she deserved, having worked hard and produced good results. She wanted to leave the company she worked for – a large investment bank. Her body language and voice conveyed uncertainty and boredom. Having worked on body language, we proceeded to use the exercises described above. I didn't need to give her any feedback on her voice – she was shocked at how bored she sounded. I took a hand-held mirror so she could see how little she used her lips and to practice stretching her mouth for the Peter Piper exercise. She thought that she would sound really silly when trying to put on an 'overly' enthusiastic/approachable/authoritative voice but was amazed at the result. She committed to purchasing her own voice recorder, practicing deep breathing, articulation in front of a mirror and voice practice on a daily basis, with great results.

Pitfalls

A coach needs to have a good range of voice themselves – so check yours out with a voice recorder.

Bibliography

Grant-Williams, R. (2002) *Voice Power: Using your Voice to Captivate, Persuade and Command Attention*, New York, NY: Amacom.

35

Multi-level modelling

Bruce Grimley

Purpose

Modelling is the skill of retrieving a coachee's 'formula' for performing a specific skill, in order that the formula can be learned by another. This is done by observing and asking questions of the person being modelled, in order to make explicit the processes they use to achieve the skill. Very often this 'formula' is totally unconscious to the coachee and bringing it more to the conscious awareness assists them to see their blind spots. Once this is achieved they are then in a position to change them quite easily. Very often, a good way of working with clients is to assist them in modelling the *unproductive* behaviour/thoughts/feelings they come to you with using what Robert Dilts called 'logical levels'. Even though it is not quite clear to some what the logical arrangement is, the model is a very useful framework for retrieving the coachee's 'formula' so they can then change it. As always with NLP, there are specific identifiable steps.

Description

In this exercise you work with the client as they explore different dimensions of a particular skill. The technique uses modelling and you will take the client through the six logical levels.

Process

1 Physically lay out one space for each of the six logical levels:

- spiritual/mission;
- identity;
- beliefs/values;
- capabilities/strategies;
- behaviours;
- environment.

2 Stand in the 'environment' space and ask the question, 'When and where do I engage in the activity to be modelled?'.

3 Stand in the 'behaviours' space and ask the question, 'What do I do when I am in those times and places?'. Notice not only the overt behaviours, but also the minimal behaviours as you take a fly on the wall perspective (third perceptual position).

4 Stand in the 'capabilities/strategies' space and ask the questions, 'How do I use my mind and physiology to carry out those behaviours?' and 'What capabilities/strategies do I have to do those actions in those times and places?'.

5 Stand in the 'beliefs/values' space and ask the questions, 'Why do I use those particular capabilities to accomplish those activities?', 'What is important to me when I am involved in those activities?', 'What beliefs guide me when I am doing them?' and 'What is the sustaining emotion that keeps me going through difficult times?'.

6 Stand in the 'identity' space and ask the question, 'Who am I when I am engaged in those beliefs, capabilities and behaviours in those times and places?'.

7 Finally, stand in the 'spiritual/purpose' space and ask the questions, 'Who else am I serving with this activity?', 'What is my mission?', 'Of what am I a part of here?' and 'What is the vision I am pursuing or representing?'.

Pitfalls

Keeping the spaces separate so you only talk about behaviour in the behaviour space and do not wander into capability or belief is important in keeping this coaching 'clean'. By separating the various levels, the coachee much more easily comes to appreciate what specifically is keeping them in their unproductive behaviour, and is then in the position to make the appropriate changes. In NLP, often we talk of 'purity of state' and 'contamination of state'. If we allow our coachee to mix up behaviour with belief or strategy, it is less clear what precisely is preventing forward movement, and therefore a focus on an appropriate change at the appropriate level.

Bibliography

Dilts, R. (1990) *Changing Belief Systems with NLP*, Capitola, CA: Meta Publications.

Dilts, R. and DeLozier, J. (2000) *Encyclopedia of Systemic Neuro-Linguistic Programming and NLP New Coding*, Scotts Valley, CA: NLP University Press.

36

Success role modelling

Diana Hogbin-Mills

Purpose

This exercise enables the creation of behaviours that the client thinks would be successful for their career development and wants to demonstrate.

Description

This exercise helps clients to get better at admired behaviours/skills that they are unsure how to achieve. The exercise will help clients to distil skills or behaviours into actions and thought processes. Forty-five minutes should be allowed for this exercise and your client may need to revisit the exercise depending on the level of observation carried out previously on a desired skill or behaviour. The client can break down the learning process into achievable steps in order to develop new skills and behaviours that have been proven to help other people achieve success.

Process

1 Identify up to three skills or behaviours that the client witnesses in other people which they believe are desirable in helping them to develop. For each skill/behaviour, distil it into a very specific action (or sequence of actions) and anticipated mind-set. Think about what they have seen, heard or experienced in their role model person when demonstrating their selected skill/behaviour, for example:

- What did you see them do when they did X, what did you notice about their body language, were there any specific hand or facial gestures that they used?
- How do you imagine they felt?
- How were they talking, what did you hear them saying, what did you notice about their tone, and volume, were there any specific intonations?

2 If needed, craft a conversation to ask the role model person what actions they are aware of when they demonstrate a particular skill/behaviour. Ideally, the questions should include a question to help guide the role model person through what it is they do when undertaking an action, for example: When you do X, what do you think, feel, see first, then what, then what, etc.

3 Identify specific steps they will undertake to master the actions and thereby skills/behaviour that they want to develop.

Pitfalls

The client may identify skills/behaviours that they value but are not valued by the business or their career influencers. There is a need, therefore, to check this. The client may find the process of modelling too complex.

Bibliography

Knight, S. (2002) *NLP at Work: The Difference that Makes a Difference in Business* (revised edition), London: Nicholas Brealey Publishing.

37

The Frame Game

Denis Gorce-Bourge

Purpose

The Frame Game is very useful in a business context, although there are situations in private life where it can be applied. It is an especially efficient strategy for someone seeking assistance with time management. It requires a comfortable setting, plus a pen and some paper.

Description

The Frame Game can help people become aware of time wasted, as opposed to time well spent. The game uses a simple drawing to demonstrate how much of their time is spent 'on-task' and how much is spent 'off-task'. The game also demonstrates that the person drawing the frame has the power to change what appears inside and outside of the frame.

For example, if your client operates a service business, it is sometimes difficult for them to put a 'frame' around the services they offer. They may want to satisfy their customers at any price and be tempted to do more than what they are paid for. They may also have accepted to provide the service at a discounted fee. They make less money and give more, resulting in burnout.

I was once using the Frame Game strategy with a team of professionals in the property business. One member of the team was spending 100 per cent of her time outside the frame and another 30 per cent of her time inside the frame. It meant many weekends and late nights at work and by spending so much time outside the frame, she was failing to deliver successful outcomes for the business.

This kind of behaviour results in a decrease in the quality of service provided, an increase in customer complaints and a decrease in income for the business. The objective of the exercise is to make the client realize what he/she is missing out on in terms of income and how much of his/her time and energy is wasted. It demonstrates that a clear, well-defined frame can ensure successful business outcomes.

Process

Give your client a piece of paper with a frame drawn in the centre of the page. The frame borders an ideal situation where the person is doing exactly what he/she is supposed to do: nothing more, nothing less. Now, ask your client to realistically draw their current situation. He/she may draw inside and outside the frame. Anything drawn inside the frame indicates what is supposed to be done, which is all good. Anything drawn outside the frame indicates what is done, but not supposed to be done, which needs consideration.

The frame places a boundary around the services the customer is paying for. Anything that appears outside the frame demonstrates how much more is being delivered and how much more your client will need to do every time to satisfy his/her customer. By wasting time doing things that he/she is not paid to do, he/she will most likely miss or forget to do the things he/she is supposed to do and provide a lower level of service, which may result in customer complaints.

At this point, you can ask your client to draw another picture (which should only take a few minutes) to demonstrate their understanding of how to ensure that services delivered are only ever those that fit neatly into the frame. Overlaps to the outside do occur, but they should be an exception.

As a coach, you will always focus your attention on what is happening on the outside of your client's frame, because fixing the outside will automatically fix the inside. If your client is spending less time doing unnecessary things, he/she will have more time to do what is expected, and more time and energy to focus correctly.

At the beginning of each session, you can ask your client to re-draw the frame to evidence the progress being made in keeping services delivered inside the frame, and those outside, to a minimum.

Pitfalls

There are no pitfalls to this strategy.

38

The swish model
Bruce Grimley

Purpose

The purpose of this exercise is to allow the client to feel positive in a situation where previously they have felt unresourceful.

Description

The swish model helps an individual identify how they are, in a way, making a mountain out of a molehill concerning a particular situation. The swish is a technique for reducing this 'mountain' again to the size of a molehill. When this happens the individual feels much more confident in being able to tackle their problems and consequently can begin to put into place the appropriate behaviours to take them to their outcome.

Process

- Ask the coachee to identify a specific behaviour that they wish to change.
- Tell them to treat the current behaviour as an achievement. If they had to teach someone how to limit themselves in this way, what would they need to see, hear and do? What would be the most salient of the senses?
- Ask the coachee to find at least two aspects of the senses that they feel are salient. For instance, if it is hearing, one aspect may be that the volume is turned up very high. If it

is vision, the other person communicating may 'appear' very large and close. This initial representation is known as the cue. Ensure that the coachee is associated (seeing/hearing out of their eyes/ears). Once you have done this, distract the coachee in some neutral exercise so that the experience to date is no longer represented in their neurophysiology.

- Now ask the coachee to represent themselves as they would really like to be in this situation. Use your language skills as a coach to ensure that the representation is as compelling as it can be and ensure that the coachee can see themselves in the picture. So, for example, the person will see themselves on the end of someone shouting at them, however they are relaxed because they have turned the volume down as they represent the auditory aspects of the communication. There may also be a visual component and in the new representation they might have also reduced the size of the person shouting at them. As a result of this distortion, the coachee might see herself as more confident as well. The picture of themselves succeeding needs also to fit in with the rest of their life; this is known as ecology in NLP.

- Now again distract the coachee for the same reason as above. This is known as 'breaking state' in NLP.

- Take the cue and make it large and loud *if those are the identified senses and critical aspects.* In the corner of this picture put a small dark, picture of the new self-image. Now change the position of the two images so the small dark one becomes large and bright, and vice versa. The visual brain works very quickly so you do not need a lot of time to do this. Make sure the old image really does fade and shrink by repeating this change as many times as necessary. This is usually 5–6. Break state after each change. This is to ensure this is a one-way ticket. A reverse swish will just cancel out a forward one. Once your coachee has broken state, repeat 5–6 times. The swish technique can be done for all of the senses; however, it is most frequently used with the visual sense.

- Ask your coachee to think of the cue. Does it elicit the same response, or does it elicit the new response? When this model is used effectively, your coachee will be amazed at how quickly a congruent different response can be elicited in such a short period of time.

Pitfalls

- Make sure the coachee totally 'breaks state' in between phases.
- Make sure the coachee is totally 'real' in each of the phases and is not just going through the motion to please you as the coach.
- Make sure the new behaviours and thoughts created through the new representation are aligned with the rest of the coachee's life and the outcomes currently being negotiated.
- Make sure the process is repeated as many times as necessary to install this new pattern. One pitfall is to only do the swish two or three times and leave it there.

Bibliography

Bandler, R. (1985) *Using your Brain – For a Change*, Boulder, CO: Real People Press.

39

Time projection imagery

Gladeana McMahon

Purpose

The purpose of this strategy is to help the client appreciate that all things pass and that life will move on regardless of how difficult a situation may seem at the present time.

Description

When facing difficult situations, it is easy for the client to lose hope, believing that life will always be difficult and this belief can lead to low mood, a sense of hopelessness and the client engaging in unhelpful behaviours.

Process

The client is asked to imagine what life might be like in six months, a year, two years or five years from now. The client is asked to consider what might have changed? The coach uses the client's past experiences and how the client has over-come previous difficult situations as a way of reinforcing the reality that life does move on even after a period of adversity.

Pitfalls

This technique does not normally have any negative con-sequences associated with it. However, it is important that this exercise is used only where the coach already has a pre-existing relationship with the client and has a considerable amount of information about the client that can be used to reinforce the concept of future positive change based on this.

Bibliography

Dryden, W., Neenan, M. and Yankurs, J. (1999) *Counselling Individuals: A Rational Emotive Behavioural Handbook*, London: Whurr.

Lazarus, A. A. (1981) *The Practice of Multimodal Therapy*, New York, NY: McGraw-Hill.

D

Focusing on the future

40

Action planning

Angela Dunbar

Purpose

The purpose of this strategy is to bring a session to a positive conclusion with realistic actions that the client can commit to.

Description

This exercise is a useful way of bringing other coaching strategies to a conclusion, particularly the Clean Language strategies. As with other Clean Language strategies, this one is particularly powerful if the client is using metaphor. It is a really great way to get an action plan – regardless of whether you've been using Clean Language previously with a client.

Process

Whatever the outcome the client is working towards, having already explored it, this exercise begins with: 'And what needs to happen for [client's outcome]?'. Repeat back what they say, then continue to ask:

'And what else needs to happen for [client's outcome]?', until they have nothing else to add. Repeat all the actions/ points made back to the client. Then ask: 'And what's the first thing that needs to happen?'. Whatever that point is, ask: 'And can . . . [client words]?'. If they say yes, move on to the next point. If they say no, ask: 'What needs to happen for [client's point]?'. Work your way through all the points made in this way.

Although it's not totally clean, I would generally end this exercise by having the client agree when they will take each action. If the client is still using metaphor you will probably find that by asking them the 'And can . . .' question, they will find an appropriate action.

Pitfalls

None.

Bibliography

Tompkins, P. and Lawley, J. (2000) *Metaphors in Mind*, London: The Developing Company Press.

41

Career choice

Diana Hogbin-Mills

Purpose

This is a 30–60 minute exercise, depending on how long a client discusses possible choices and actions to assist the client's viewpoint about possible directions they can take and avoiding having all their eggs in one basket.

Description

This exercise prompts a 'big picture conversation' about the client's next aspired job or career move. It encourages the client to open up and share thoughts on possible career ideas. It is especially helpful if a client is only considering a job or career move in one direction. It explores multiple ideas for each of the career options (boxes) so if one option does not work out, they still have other options and a momentum to move forward.

Process

1 Create a template, or ask the client to draw a two-by-two grid, getting them to add four labels and descriptors for each box, as shown in Figure 4.
2 Check that the client understands the meaning of each box. Use the following prompts to clarify their understanding:

 • **Stabilize** – if they are relatively new to a role and/or feel that they still have a lot to achieve in their current

SEARCH . . . For a new role within your existing organization	STRETCH . . . For a new role in a new organization
STABILIZE . . . Stay in the existing organization and in the same role	SHIFT . . . To a new organization doing the same role

Figure 4 Career choice exercise

position, including developing skills that are essential for the next move. Typical if in role for less than one to two years.

- **Search** – look in their existing organization for a new role as they would the external job market. It should be easier to move internally and transfer skills to a new position than in the external market, especially if they have a good reputation.

- **Shift** – consider a new organization if they enjoy what they do but there is not a good fit with the organizational culture or they want to work in a different location or industry. This might also be a good stepping-stone into a stretch role.
- **Stretch** – change everything about their job. This type of move is likely to take the longest to achieve and probably requires the most effort and preparation.

3 Ask the client to talk about their likely career choices, based on the grid. Jot down what they would like to do, allocating it to one of the boxes – boxes can have multiple job options. Encourage them to share all their job thoughts no matter how usual or unusual they are.

4 Invite the client to identify their preferred two to three career choices and order of priority. Why? Explain ... Multiple career options spread the risk of career development. If they only have one option and it is closed off then they will feel stunted and frustrated. More than one option increases the chances of being able to take action, gain results and move in a new direction. Ask the client to identify short-, medium- and long-term actions for each career choice.

Case study

A client came to coaching having been in their current role for two to three years doing something that they were doing more because of necessity than love or interest. They decided that it really was time for a change. We used the career choices grid to talk about the direction(s) they wanted to move to. Up to that point they had only thought about a stretch move. We talked about the benefits of developing multiple career options and identifying a range of quick wins to kick off their career development as well as set up actions for their long-term (and harder) career development moves. As a result, the client started to have conversations with their manager about the types of tasks they enjoyed and how they could do more of them (which were also their strength areas), as well as the opportunity for an internal promotion. Within the next few months the client earned an internal promotion when previously they had been told there was not any opportunity for promotion. Why? They had demonstrated by shifting their role slightly to play more to their strengths how much they could contribute to the business, and the business was able to reward that when an opportunity came along.

Pitfalls

A client may not want to take the time to consider multiple career options and push forward with a move out of a company.

Bibliography

Kaye, B. (1997) *Up is NOT the Only Way* (revised edition), Boston, MA: Davies-Black.

Career visioning

Diana Hogbin-Mills

Purpose

This strategy creates a vision for what a client's future, particularly their career, may look like and identifies actions needed in the short, medium and long term to realize it.

Description

Taking control is an empowering state to be in. This exercise enables the client to take control of their career and make a plan for the future. It will prompt them to think about their ideal career future and from there they can identify short-, medium- and long-term goals.

Process

1 Create a template using a piece of A4 paper or bigger, turned so the longest edge is at the bottom. Divide the page into four by folding the page into half then half again. This will create four columns. Write the headings 'next year', '2 years', '5 years' and '10 years', one to each column, as shown in Figure 5.

Invite the client to put themselves in a relaxed state (for example, take a few deep breaths, sit comfortably, etc.) and imagine their life stretching out before them. Start by gathering personal information about their life in the future, for example where do they want to be living, and then add in career-related information. *Reassure them that*

Next year	2 years	5 years	10 years

Figure 5 **Career visioning exercise**

while you are going to be asking them questions about their future, they can choose what they write down and they can share with you only what they feel comfortable doing.

It is unlikely that all clients will be able to project out to 10 years for all or some of the visioning questions but encourage them to fill in what they can and invite them to keep adding to it over time. They may need to go away and do some additional thinking on some categories (for example how much income they want/need) but you can still complete the majority of the exercise.

2 Fill in their template using the following personal questions:

- How old will you be next year, in two years' time etc.?
- What will be your expected/hoped for relationship/

family status in the next year, two years' time, etc.? (e.g. children, preschool, married, divorced, etc.)

- What will be your expected/hoped for living status in a year's time, two years' time, etc.? (e.g. in the same accommodation; if not, what will it be)
- What will be your expected/hoped for location next year, in two years' time, etc.? (e.g. same area)
- What will be your expected/hoped for income next year, in two years' time, etc.?
- What physical shape do you want/hope to have next year, in two years' time, etc.?

3 Next, invite them to add career information to each of the defined categories. Example questions include the following (choose ones that will be most relevant to your client):

- What type of employment would you like to have next year, in two years' time, etc.? (full-time, part-time, consultancy)
- Would you like it to be the same or different from now? How will it change over the years?
- What type of company/industry would you like to be working for next year, in two years' time, etc.? Would you like it to be the same or different from now?
- What size of company would you like to be working in the next year, in two years' time, etc.?
- What type of work will you be doing next year, in two years' time, etc.?
- What level will you be working at next year, in two years' time, etc.? (e.g. manager, board member, advisor, etc.)
- What location would you like to be working from next year, in two years' time, etc.? Would you like it to be the same or different from now?
- What type of people would you like to be working with next year, in two years' time, etc.?
- How many jobs/roles do you think you will have had in the next year, in two years, etc.?
- What type of environment will you be working in next year, in two years' time, etc.? (e.g. office based, home worker, mobile)

- What hours will you be working next year, in two years' time, etc.?
- What will you be known for at your work?
- What skills will you be utilizing next year, in two years' time, etc.? (e.g. specific skills or more generally; existing skills or new skills, etc.)
- What behaviours will you be demonstrating in the next year, in two years' time, etc. that will be most effective in helping you to achieve what you want?
- What will you have achieved from a career next year, in two years' time, etc.?
- What skills will you be developing in the next year, in two years' time, etc.?

4 Once completed, invite the client to reflect on what comes to mind when they review their career future – discuss, add, edit information, etc. Identify short-, medium- and long-term actions to help them achieve their career life stage aspirations. The client will feel empowered. They can be proactive in managing their career and create opportunities.

Pitfalls

A client may not want to or be able to think ahead to what they are going to do in the future, preferring instead to work with opportunities as they come up.

Bibliography

Bergman Fortgang, L. (2005) *Take Yourself to the Top*, New York, NY: Tarcher-Penguin.

Martin, C. (2001) *The Life Coaching Handbook: Everything You Need to Be an Effective Life Coach*, Carmarthen: Crown House Publishing.

43

Future vision

Christine K. Champion

Purpose

This exercise is introduced to the client in a coaching session but is best completed away from the coaching as a creative writing homework activity. The exercise encourages visualization techniques to encourage the client to look into the future – say, 10 years ahead or a meaningful timescale for the individual – and to retrospectively review their most notable achievements and contributions. What is their legacy?

Description

This exercise encourages the client to create a written legacy as if they were a third party. It taps into their creativity and can be done either in a coaching session or as homework.

Process

The process provides clarity through the creative writing process and can provide some real insights to support the client in assessing and designing their future professional role. The piece is written by the client in the role of a third person, say a journalist in a relevant professional publication, who writes a professional profile of the client's achievements 10 years from now.

Encourage the client to prepare a relaxing and uninterrupted environment to write the piece (phones off!), giving the instructions/asking the questions that follow:

- Play your favourite music, relax, and design the writing environment to help you to feel at one with yourself.
- Consider your future vision of your ideal career path, where would you like to be and what would you like to achieve in 5/10 years' time.
- How will you have made a difference? What are the key events?
- Take some time to visualize this. What will you look like? What will it feel like? What will be around you? What will you be doing?
- Be careful not to be judgemental while visualizing your future self.
- If appropriate for you, consider your family, important others and life-balance issues. Start writing – get into the flow and let your creative juices form the story. Do not judge or moderate the content of the piece.

The client should then bring the article to the next coaching session and the coach's role is to draw out key insights revealed in the writing and to provide reflective space:

- How important is this to you?
- How would you feel/what would you think if you were to achieve this accolade?
- How serious are you about this?
- What actions can you take to start moving forward?

Pitfalls

Not all individuals will feel comfortable with this exercise and may be unable or unwilling to harness their internal creativity for this purpose.

44

The new behaviour generator

Bruce Grimley

Purpose

The purpose of this strategy is literally to do what it says on the tin, and that is to generate new behaviours that have not hitherto been a part of an individual's repertoire.

Description

We are *all excellent at doing some things* and this is because our experiences have trained us to filter sensory information in such a way that is unique to us. Conversely, there are some behaviours that, however much we try, seem to elude us when it comes to the crunch. The new behaviour generator is a coaching strategy that helps us alter the way we currently look at the world so we can get that same confident feeling we all can relate to, when we try the things we would like to do, but at the moment can't.

The strategy takes advantage of the fact that our unconscious minds do not differentiate real from imagined data. If you like steak and begin to think about having one, seeing it cooked just how you like it, with your favourite trimmings, as you do sensing the wonderful aroma, with the heat radiating up from the fresh serving, anticipating biting into the freshly cooked meat and tasting those familiar juices . . . you begin to activate all the neurotransmitters and chemical messengers as if you really were actually eating a steak. The new behaviour generator is like a simulator, which allows you to experience yourself in the future and then to make the necessary alterations so you can be who you wish to be and feel great about it.

The TOTE presented in Figure 6 shows how this coaching strategy has as its main focus what we see ourselves doing in the future and how we feel about this (TOTE – Test, Operate, Test and Exit; see Miller et al., 1960). We negotiate the visual sensory information and the feelings generated as we 'act out' and communicate this back in a loop. We eventually obtain a congruent picture of us doing and being just who we wish to be, on our terms, aligned with our important personal values.

Process

1 Ask the client to think of a time when they were wonderfully confident and very successful. Ask them to experience that fully, making a note of specifically where and how they experience the feelings.
2 Then direct the client to ask themselves: 'If I had already achieved my goal, what is it I would look like? How would I sound, who and what would surround me, how would I relate to that environment?'. Strategies to aid this step are:

- breaking the goal down into steps and seeing themselves doing the initial steps;
- modelling someone who can achieve their outcome well;
- remembering a previous achievement where they effectively accomplished an outcome and modelling their physiology, tonality and environment at that time;

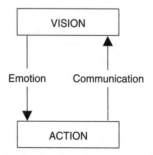

Figure 6 A TOTE

- creating a line on the floor with the future at one end, the present in the middle and the past at the other end; then using this as a spatial representation of time.

3 When you think the client has got the representation as compelling as they can, invite them to step into the representation and experience themselves succeeding in their outcome.
4 When the client has spent some time doing this, invite them to compare the feelings they have at this time of the strategy to the feelings from step 1 when they experienced *knowing* they were very successful.
5 If the feelings are the same, the strategy is complete. If the feelings are not the same, ask the client to verbalize what else it is they need in order to be successful in achieving their outcome. After doing this, go back to step 2 and repeat the process.

Pitfalls

- Working with perceptual positions (that is, seeing yourself from a fly on the wall perspective, or becoming fully you by *only* experiencing the world through your senses) and other NLP techniques like working with time lines and modelling, are strategies that take time to develop competence in. Do not be discouraged if using this strategy seems a bit weird at first for either you or your client. There are plenty of good resources on the world wide web to assist you to more fully understand these, and with time you will feel more comfortable with the strategies and the associated language.
- When doing step 1, make sure the client generates very specific locations in their body, and other specific aspects of feeling, and then test these by feeding these aspects back to them and noticing what effect this has on their physiology. This is important as later this state is used as a comparison.
- When comparing states of confidence at stage 4, the feelings may be textured differently. The importance of the comparison is to ensure the intensity and level of the new

confidence generated by what they see is the same as when they *know* they have been confident in the past.

Bibliography

Dilts, R. and Epstein, T. (1991) *Tools for Dreamers*, Capitola, CA: Meta Publications.

45

Visualizing future goals: back to the future

Gill Dickers

Purpose

Promoting lifelong learning and encouraging the ability to transfer skills are now part of many organizational and university programmes. The 'what next?' question must be dealt with. Supported by fellow participants and the coaching process, the following activity uses drama to help to articulate dreams, and make plans to achieve these.

Description

The session facilitates the exploration of life and work goals. The activity is recommended for groups of about 12 who have worked together over a period of time. It is advisable to only use the techniques on courses where drama and movement have been integral, or where there is a commitment to using creative methods, for example, on play work, youth and community work, counselling, mental health nursing and social work courses. Themes on the human and, hence, student condition, such as futures, choice, change and hope, can be dramatically explored by using traditional story telling structures, as outlined by Gersie and King (1990).

Materials required are relaxing music and some simple props.

Process

I have identified five steps for the strengths and skills strategy:

1 **Warm up**: The session uses warm-up techniques, which will give participants the language of the session, for example, a physical activity, where they meet and greet each other. Rules of engagement and confidentiality are also agreed. The session uses techniques drawn from neurolinguistic programming and drama.

2 **Visualization**: After the warm-up, students are asked to sit and, if this feels comfortable, to close their eyes. Relaxing music can help the process. They should consider the year(s) ahead and imagine they have reached their ideal day. The leader can put forward the following questions:

   • When they wake up where will they be?
   • What are the sounds?
   • What will they feel?
   • What will they choose to wear?
   • What will be the first thing they notice?
   • What will others notice about them?

3 **The journey**: At an appropriate time, the participants are asked to work with a partner. One person is the director, the other describes their dream. The director asks the dreamer to visualize an event in their ideal day, imagine a journey from the present that will take them to this event. With the director's support, the dreamer walks slowly towards the imagined place whilst describing the journey. As they arrive, the director asks the dreamer to turn and look back at the starting point of the journey and say what he, or she, sees, feels and thinks. What support and advice do they give to themselves? They should walk back to the starting place and look back at the future and be encouraged to discuss their observations, feelings and new realizations. After discussion, the roles can be reversed.

4 **Reflection**: It is important that time is allocated for whole group sharing and private reflection. Each member should be given the opportunity to debrief from the activity, to say what worked and did not work, and to thank their director.

5 **The plans**: They should then make their individual plans, sharing one step that will take them towards these. They

leave as individuals, not as group members, taking their individual thoughts and plans with them.

Pitfalls

This is a powerful group exercise. The group leader needs to be experienced in the use of drama with groups and able to create, and sustain, safe working spaces. This is not recommended if people have had unsafe group experiences in the past, and/or if the group is a new group.

Bibliography

Gersie, A. and King, N. (1990) *Storymaking in Education and Therapy*, London: Jessica Kingsley.
Johnstone, K. (1981) *Impro: Improvisation and the Theatre*, London: Methuen.
O'Connor, J. and Lages, A. (2002) *Coaching with NLP: A Practical Guide to Getting the Best out of Yourself and Others*, London: Element, HarperCollins.

E

Group coaching

46

Box process

David Adams

Purpose

This strategy has been developed from work done over the past 50 years by members of Vistage International (formerly TEC International). Vistage is the leading world-wide membership organization for managing directors and chief executives.

The strategy has been successfully transferred from the SME (Small and Medium Enterprises) sector into group coaching for senior executive teams including boards and middle management teams in both national and multi-national organizations and corporations. (Suggested time: 45 minutes.)

The exercise enables larger groups of people to process, simultaneously, a greater number of issues than would normally be possible within standard time frames. Total time: up to 40–60 minutes depending on group size. *(Based on a format devised by Vistage USA Resource Speaker, Larry Wilson.)*

Description

This exercise provides the ability to process a considerable number of issues with a larger group in a relatively short time.

Process

1 Have each participant select the **Strategic Initiative** where they are making the least progress or simply their most burning key issue.

(a) Have everyone take a clean sheet of paper and draw a large box – 4″ × 6″ to 5″ × 7″ in the middle of the paper (see Figure 7).

(b) Have them take **2 minutes** to write their story in the box in bullet form:

- beliefs about it;
- limitations they face;
- expectations they have;

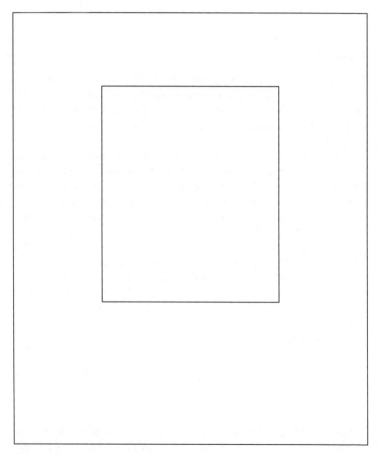

Figure 7 Box process exercise

- challenges;
- their opinions;
- their reasons;
- their judgements – about others, themselves, the situation;
- etc.

2 Break the participants into groups of three or four, depending on total group size.

    (a) Set the chairs so that they are close together, facing each other.

    (b) They will need something hard to write on like a pad or notebook.

3 Process

    (a) Have each group pick an 'A'.

    (b) Have the person to A's left go first.

    (c) Have that person share their story with the others – **2 minutes**.

    (d) *STOP* (the facilitator will have to be pushy about stopping . . .).

    (e) Have the person who just shared, turn his/her chair around – back to the others.

    (f) Have the two or three others brainstorm the topic as if the person with their back turned is not there. Talk with each other, not to the person – **4 minutes**.

    (g) The person with their back turned does not speak, simply listens for new ideas, approaches, etc. and writes them on their paper outside the box.

    (h) *STOP*.

    (i) Have the person turn their chair back around and share what they just heard or learned – **1 minute**.

    (j) *STOP*.

    (k) Acknowledge each other (this is a vital part of the process).

    (l) Repeat the process until everyone has had a turn – **21–28 minutes**.

4 Debrief

    (a) Bring everyone back together.

(b) Ask the participants to share what it was like to have their back turned and just to listen:

- How did it feel?
- What did they notice about themselves?
- Etc.

(c) Ask the participants to share what it was like to be talking about the topic 'behind the person's back'.

(d) Work with the group on what they learned about communication, how long it takes to present and work an issue, what cherished beliefs they had about communication that were blown away by their experience, etc.

(e) Complete – capture learnings – **15–20 minutes**.

Pitfalls

Careful and skilled facilitation is required.

47

Disruptive thinking/disruptive marketing

David Adams

Purpose

This is a group exercise where members of the group are singled out to be tested by the rest of their colleagues in relation to identifying disruptive thinking and disruptive marketing implications.

Description

The exercise is totally conceptual. The individuals in the group are made to consider the implications of a disruption of business from influences wholly outside of their control. The technique can be modified to enable it to be used as a marketing strategy. This exercise uses the power of the group to stretch the minds and thinking of its members.

Process

Examples for disruptive thinking

1 A house builder in the south-east of England is forced to build houses without using water due to extreme drought conditions. This scenario forces the subject to think differently. By using this process, accepting that the scenario is highly unlikely, it forces the thinking to be thoroughly creative. Even if a solution to the problem is discovered, this is not the point of the exercise because other aspects of the business in question will be forced into the open.

2 Newspaper publisher forced to reconsider business model due to total unavailability of newsprint.
3 Fish importer who supplies supermarkets finds all sources of fish have disappeared from the seas or has been totally contaminated with mercury.
4 Government minister decrees that no private transport is to be used for the carriage of goods.

Examples for disruptive marketing

These are based on real examples from well-known industries:

1 Apple inventing the iPod, completely overshadowing the Sony Walkman.
2 Dyson inventing the bagless vacuum cleaner.
3 Ryanair charging passengers for baggage; now charging passengers to check in physically rather than online.

Groups can work in twos or threes to brainstorm new ideas and create 'new products' or can work together as a complete group. In addition to the traditional brainstorm process, Edward De Bono's *Six Thinking Hats* process can be used.

Pitfalls

The group needs to be able to be free-thinking but, indeed, that is the purpose of these exercises.

Bibliography

de Bono, E. (2000) *Six Thinking Hats* (2nd revised edition), London: Penguin.
Gilbert, I. (2004) *Little Owl's Book of Thinking: An Introduction to Thinking Skills*, Carmarthen: Crown House Publishing.
Kerin, R. and Peterson, R. (2006) *Strategic Marketing Problems: Cases and Comments*, London: Prentice Hall.

48

Issue processing

David Adams

Purpose

This is a simple but extremely effective process to get the
most out of an individual's issue, using the combined experience and wisdom of the group to reach an optimum solution.

Description

The issue holder is invited to state succinctly the issue s/he
wishes to resolve, what the ideal outcome would look like,
what they have done about it to date and what help they
would like from the group. Where appropriate, the raiser of
the issue is asked to ascribe a monetary value thereto. This
part of the exercise should be allowed to take no more than
three to four minutes. This is a very powerful process, enabling group wisdom to be focused on one group member's
issue.

Process

The group then begins to ask clarifying questions to elicit
a clear understanding of the problem. Under no circumstances may any member be permitted to introduce a solution at this stage by framing a solution in the guise of a
question (for example, 'Have you thought about doing . . .?').

Questioning continues until the group feels that it
really understands what is going on – the skilled facilitator/
coach will know instinctively when this point has been

reached. The facilitator will then ask a member of the group to restate the issue. It is often the case that the originally verbalized issue is not the underlying one. The clarifying questions will have enabled the real issue to be exposed. Often the issue is about relationships; thus, an issue about the performance of a direct report can often turn out to be about the leadership skills of the manager. This part of the process should be allocated the bulk of the time available (at least 30 minutes).

Once the issue has been restated and reframed if necessary, the group will go into solution mode. Each member will, in turn, proffer advice – ideally, members will build on what has already been said and members may be asked to go out of turn if they wish to 'piggy-back' on what has just been said. The piggy-back process is also encouraged during the clarification stage. During the solution stage the issue holder keeps silent, avoiding such obvious reactions as 'We've tried that – it doesn't work.'

Once all the solutions have been voiced and a few moments taken for reflection, the issue holder responds with what s/he has heard, feeds back the viability of the ideas presented and finally tells the assembly the actions that will be taken next. A commitment to report back to next meeting of the group is requested and acknowledged.

A variation on the direct solution mode is where the group voices concerns for the issue holder – particularly powerful in poor trading conditions that have not been identified or acted upon properly; this can then be followed by a round of 'on the other hand, I see an opportunity'.

Pitfalls

The process requires able and skilful facilitation.

49

Leading as a team

Anne Archer

Purpose

The purpose of this strategy is to enable a leadership team to have clarity about their effectiveness and the impact they have on their business.

Description

Most leadership development will focus on individual leaders. Often the description leadership team is used to describe a loose collection of individuals who come together to agree strategy and monitor progress. By exploring the purpose of a leadership team with an emphasis on the 'team', effectiveness and impact can be considerably enhanced.

Process

It is essential for all members of the leadership team to be present for the session. The leadership coach needs to be able to challenge defensive answers whilst creating an open and honest environment. The first step is to establish what leadership means to individuals within the group. It is usual to have three broad areas of strategic direction and communication, change management and team performance. Keep it simple. The most important part of the process is the quality of the discussion. Suggest that they ask the following questions about themselves as a team:

Strategic direction

- What do we do as a team to determine the strategy?
- How do we know everyone in the team is truly bought in?
- What is the purpose of the team in achieving the strategy?
- How do we set team goals that are aligned to the vision?
- How do we leverage our collective knowledge/wisdom?

Change management

- How do we as a team balance ambiguity and certainty?
- What does our team leadership style say to our staff about what we value?
- How inclusive are we as a team?
- What changes are we expecting and how do we make them stick?

Team performance

- What do we need to shift to optimise our team leadership impact?
- What measures are in place, or need to be in place, to ensure we are performing well as a team?
- How do we demonstrate high-performing team behaviours?
- How do we learn as a team?

For each question, be clear that as coach you get a sense of how they think, feel and act, as a team. Your goal is to help the leaders to recognise the difference between their own leadership and leadership as part of a leadership team. Once you have built a collective picture of the team, rephrase the questions to illicit how they would like the answer to be.

The gap between intention and the current reality provides useful data as part of a development plan.

Pitfalls

Be aware that the above questions can evoke defensive behaviour. Use when you have developed your own coaching skills and have an understanding of group and team dynamics.

Bibliography

Bourne, M. and Bourne, P. (2002) *Change Management in a Week*, London: Hodder & Stoughton.

Goleman, D. with Boyatzis, R. and Mckee, A. (2002) *The New Leaders*, New York, NY: Time Warner Book Group.

Kotter, J. P. (1999) *What Leaders Really Do*, Cambridge, MA: Harvard Business School Press.

Slater, R. (2003) *29 Leadership Secrets from Jack Welch*, Maidenhead: McGraw-Hill.

50

More/less/stop[1]

David Adams

Purpose

This strategy has been developed from work done over the past 50 years by members of Vistage International (formerly TEC International). Vistage is the leading world-wide membership organization for managing directors and chief executives. The strategy has been successfully transferred from the SME (small- and medium-sized enterprises) sector into group coaching for senior executive teams including boards and middle management teams in both national and multinational organizations and corporations.

It is a group exercise aimed at leading to more clarity for the individual members of the group and to greater understanding of each other. The exercise may be used as a precursor to both individual and group goal-setting.

Description

This exercise is a very effective process for clarifying individuals' needs within and without the group/team context and can be adapted for use as a one-to-one process. Where members of a team know each other reasonably well, each identifies for the other team members the following:

- what they should do more of;
- what they should do less of;
- what they should STOP doing.

Average time for the exercise – depending on group size – is

60 minutes. Where group members have insufficient information about each other and/or use the strategy as a team
building exercise, the following process can be followed (this
is particularly valid as a year-end/year-beginning exercise
but does not have to be restricted in timing.

Process

1 Group members are asked to write a brief description of
who they are (sentences, bullet points and short para-
graphs). There is one condition: *nouns are not to be used*.
This will give rise to much agonizing as individuals work
past 'what' they are to 'who' and 'how' they are. The group
then shares its findings.
2 Next, based on the description they wrote, group members
are asked to write the answers to three questions:

- What do I plan to *stop* doing in the new year?
- What do I plan to do *more* of in the new year?
- What do I plan to do *less* of in the new year?

These thoughts are then shared around the group.
3 Each member is then granted *eight free hours* during the
working week and asked to write down what they would do
with those eight free hours (Note: these are not new or
extra hours; eight of their hours are magically freed up
during the week). These thoughts are then shared around
the group.
4 The group is then told that those free hours are rescinded
and that they must still do the things they just created and
shared. The group members are then asked to write down
what eight hours worth of activities they will give up during the working week to make room for the new stuff they
came up with in step 3. This is a hard task. The thoughts
are then shared with the group.
5 Finally, it is suggested to the group that none of them will
be successful with the 'STOP doing' stuff. They will look
puzzled. They are reminded that the stuff on their STOP
list has been there for several years, and why would any-
one believe they will stop now? Then it is suggested that if
they really want results with their STOP list, they must

convert it to a START list ... we give up things when we have something else (hopefully better) with which to replace the vanquished activity. They then write, and share, the added START items.

6 These should be codified as SMART goals, if appropriate.

Pitfalls

There are no pitfalls as long as the group takes the exercise seriously and follows up after the session.

Note

1 Based on a concept from Vistage US Chairs, Larry Cassidy, Don Riddell, Vistage US Resource Speaker Bob Thomson et al.

51

Unlocking creativity

David Adams

Purpose

This strategy consists of the use of poetry to enable team members to open up to themselves and, in the process, to each other. The result is an increase in innovation and, where appropriate, greater ability to indulge in productive conflict and create greater trust.

Description

In five years of leading the process, the writer has never ceased to be amazed at the quality of output from people who claim never to have written a word since their school days. The process can be used in one-to-one coaching but is much more powerful if used in a group setting.

Process

First, the mood needs to be set by the judicious reading of some motivational or emotive poem by the facilitator. Examples might be *Faith* by David Whyte; *Once More unto the Breach, Dear Friends* from Henry V; *Love After Love* by Derek Walcott. This can be a basic 30-minute exercise or taken as part of a 90-minute or three-hour workshop (see also www.unlocking-creativity.com).

Group members are then asked to consider a situation or issue that they want/need to change. They make bullet-point notes under a column headed *Present Reality* (see

Figure 8). Having been given a few minutes *(maximum five minutes)*, they are then asked to bullet point, not necessarily in parallel, their *Future Reality*, their Ideal Outcome. They are told that at no stage will they be asked to share the contents of these two columns. They are warned that they will, however, be asked to share the contents of a third, middle column.

Once they have completed *Present Reality* and *Future Reality*, the delegates are asked to put one word in a central column – that is, one word only, not one word for each bullet point – and are told that they should write down the first word that comes into their head, not the one that comes in after they discard the first. They must follow their 'gut'. They are asked to write down the word that is stopping them getting from *Present Reality* to *Future Reality*. (As a precursor to this exercise and subject to the time available, the group can be asked to brainstorm motivational words and then inhibiting words – this has the effect of loosening them up and acts as an 'inclusion exercise'.)

Once they have discovered their chosen word, each person must write the following at the top of a fresh page: I want

Present Reality	The chosen word here	Future Reality

Figure 8 Unlocking creativity exercise

to write about _____. In the blank space they should insert their chosen word. Words that most often come up are *cash*, *time*, *fear*, etc. They are then told to write a poem, of which the first line is: I want to write about [xxxxx]. They are informed that their poem does not need to rhyme, it does not need to scan, it just needs to follow their breathing; they just need to let it flow. They are given no more than *12–15 minutes* to do their poem.

Once written, the poems are shared. The experienced facilitator will judge how to encourage the group members to share even if they have inhibitions. Once everyone has shared their poems, they should be asked to take them away, type or write them up and meditate upon the contents. Alternatively, the members can be split into twos or threes and co-coach each other on the meaning.

Pitfalls

Care needs to be taken to ensure 'buy-in' by the participants and an agreement to complete the process all the way through. There also needs to be a willingness to open up to the other group members.

F

Problem solving
and creativity

52

Finding your niche (using Clean Language)

Angela Dunbar

Purpose

To help a client begin to explore future career directions and become more aware of what they do best. This is a less structured exercise and the client could take you anywhere with it!

Description

This exercise works best if you ask the client to prepare in advance. With this strategy, we help the client to access their metaphoric descriptions by having them draw something on a piece of paper.

Process

Depending on the context, you'd set them a preparation question: 'When you are working at your best, that's like what?'. (You can replace the word 'working' with another word to make it more appropriate to whatever they are working on.) The client's drawing then enables you to ask questions of all the metaphors that come up. You can explore how they see themselves by asking: 'And when [client's description of working at their best], whereabouts are you?' and then: 'What kind of "you" is that "you"?'. Stay within the metaphors if you can, paying attention to what the client is interested in.

A good, fail-safe question to use during this exercise is:

'And what are you drawn to now?'. Ask simple questions of all the different elements that form parts of their picture. You can help the client see how all the pieces fit together by asking 'relationship' questions. For example, 'And when you are dancing, and the tree is growing, is there a relationship between the growing tree and the dancing "you"?'. Or if the scenario is changing as the client is describing it you could ask, for example: 'And when that flower opens up, what happens to the small round ball of fire?'.

Five minutes before you end the session, ask: 'What do you know now about working at your best?' and 'And what difference does that knowing make?'.

Pitfalls

This is a less structured exercise and the client could take you anywhere with it.

Bibliography

Sullivan, W. and Rees, J. (2008) *Clean Language: Revealing Metaphors and Opening Minds*, Carmarthen: Crown House Publishing.

53

Job decision making

Diana Hogbin-Mills

Purpose

This exercise provides structured thinking to help the client come to a conclusion. More often than not, if they have come to a coach to help them with the decision they are very stuck and need an independent input to guide them through and dig down to articulate the blockers. For example, a client did not want to leave his post because he felt a great loyalty to his team but once he had identified this as his blocker he was able to put in place actions that would ensure that he felt they would be well cared for. The exercise helps to facilitate the decision about whether or not to accept a job offer.

Description

The exercise helps to bring to the surface all the reasons why a client is having difficulty deciding whether they should stay in their current job or leave. It puts a sense of priority around the reasons. It values emotional as well as rational reasons for leaving/staying. By going through this process a client can dig down and articulate powerful but previously unspoken reasons and decide what action to take.

Process

1 In this exercise you are aiming to identify the reasoning and thinking behind a client looking for a new job. It gets the client to talk about the situation.

2 For each job opportunity, create a template using a piece of A4 paper or bigger and turn it so that looking at it the shortest edge is at the bottom. Fold the page in half. Create two columns on each half of the paper by drawing a line down the page two thirds from the middle and then two thirds from the right hand side edge. Add the headings as shown in Table 1. Invite the client to list 5–10 reasons to stay in their current job and 5–10 reasons to leave the existing job and go to the new opportunity. Ask the client to prioritize their choices.

3 Take the two biggest reasons for staying or going. Compare them: does one outweigh the other? If yes, does that help with the decision-making process? If a 'yes, but' or 'no', check to see if the reasons for going are big enough. Review the biggest reason for staying. Explore in what way it is holding back progress to the new job. Check whether it is the biggest blocker to making a decision to go – clarify what is you can use metaphors, Clean Language techniques, etc. to help illicit blockers. Brainstorm ways to remove the blockage or diminish its hold (this may also include reframing the client's thinking about the situation). If they are still having difficulty deciding, go back and explore the reasons they have already stated, and challenge them on what they have written. Have they stated the real reason? Are there other underlying reasons they need to share? Do they need to edit/refine any of the reasons?

4 If the client decides to go, identify ways of getting elements of the biggest stay factor achieved through outside

Table 1 Job decision-making exercise

Reasons to stay	Priority	Reasons to go	Priority
• Strategic role	2	• No work/life balance currently	1
• Like the people	3	• New challenges	2
• Don't want to let team down	1	• Lack of support currently	3
• etc.		• etc.	

interests. If the client decides to stay, identify possible ways of getting more of their go factors.

Pitfalls

If a client is having difficult deciding, it may take more than one session to get them to a point where they are ready to share/know themselves what the possible reasons are for why they want to stay or go, which are acting as the blockers to their decision-making process.

Bibliography

Lore, N. (1998) *The Pathfinder*, Chagrin Falls, OH: Fireside.

54

Letting them draw their own conclusions

Julia Cusack

Purpose

The purpose of this strategy is to unleash creativity and/or illuminate something that is out of awareness. In the world of business today, successful people are often intellectually competent and highly skilled in rational, analytical thinking. These cerebral types are well practised at expressing themselves logically. However, using logic does not always provide the best solution. In addition, our society's over-emphasis on the written word as the primary vehicle of information in education compounds this left-brain tendency. This exercise serves to stimulate the right brain.

Description

In this exercise the client is invited to use drawing as a technique to explore an issue. The reason why, to quote the old adage, pictures are worth a thousand words, is that they make use of a massive range of cortical skills, particularly right brain: colour, form, line, dimensions, texture, visual rhythm and especially imagination. The exercise allows the individual to mentally step out of their usual way of thinking and can provide them with surprising insights. I have used this successfully with many people, not just those who predominantly favour their 'visual' and/or 'kinaesthetic' senses.

Process

Notice when it may be a pertinent time to use drawing as an intervention. Examples of indicators include:

• tracing (on the table or in the air) with their finger(s);
• using expressions that indicate preference for a visual representation system but which indicate a lack of clarity such as: 'I just can't see what he's doing' or 'I'd like to shed some light on the matter';
• appearing well-rehearsed and knowledgeable in their 'story', but keep talking round in circles.

The process is as follows:

1 Provide a large piece of paper, coloured pens, chalks, pencils and colourful stickers.
2 Invite the client to use whatever appeals to them from the available materials to create a visual representation of the situation they have been describing.
3 Encourage them to use different colours and textures to draw images, symbols or even words if necessary.
4 Many people believe, mistakenly, that they are incapable of drawing. Therefore, reassure them that it is not the quality of the drawing, but the impact on their thinking that matters.
5 Don't judge or make observations about their drawing at first; encourage them to provide a commentary as they go.
6 Pay particular attention to the words they use in their commentary, not just the drawing itself. They may well provide you with different insights as they are distracted by the activity, often revealing new patterns.
7 Continue the coaching session using the commentary and the drawing.
8 Once they have finished the picture, ask them: 'Having drawn this picture, what is your sense now of [the issue] ?'
9 Finally, ask them to review how helpful the activity was to them.

Pitfalls

The client may be embarrassed to draw with someone watching them. Most people can be encouraged to participate so it is worth spending time reassuring them (see point 4 above). However, if it is clear that they are too inhibited at this time, it may be more helpful to suggest doing the exercise privately, outside the coaching session. This has a different emphasis as you cannot bring contemporaneous observation to the exercise but is still a worthwhile activity.

55

Mind mapping for insight and problem solving based on the work of Tony Buzan

Christine K. Champion

Purpose

This exercise aims to remove barriers to lateral thinking and support the production of creative solutions and encourages holistic insight into the impact of change in one area and the knock-on effects. It also provides a structure for creative thinking and releases energy and insights.

Description

The mind map is a visual way of perceiving the world.

Process

First, outline the process of mind mapping. That it is a natural expression of radiant thinking – a natural function of the mind, it is a universal key to unlocking the brain's potential. It puts a subject/issue in the centre, with main themes radiating out from the central image as branches – all connected. Related topics of lesser importance are also represented as branches attached to higher-level branches. Encourage the client to leave the mind as free as possible to make associations and connections. This will help the client to remove internal barriers to thinking and creativity. The branches form a connected nodal structure.

The advantages of mind mapping are that it:

- keeps the whole picture in view at all times;
- provides a balanced and comprehensive understanding of the entire subject;
- increases the brain's 'hunger' for knowledge and problem solving;
- enhances understanding and appreciation of systemic linkages.

The role of the coach is to assist initially in producing a clearer picture of the situation/problem that requires resolution. So tell me about the issue? What exactly is the nature of the issue? What is it that makes it important/challenging? Who else is involved? Once the issue is clearly defined it can be plotted at the centre of the page and the mind mapping process begins by drawing out the various components of the problem. So tell me about the issues involved in this? The linkages and joined-up nature of issues really stand out on the page when presented in this manner.

Pitfalls

Some clients are not comfortable with this form of radiant thinking and prefer to view issues in a more linear manner. It can often be worth persevering with the mind map and encouraging the client to give it a go, but if the client will not engage then review the issue in a more linear format of the client's choice.

Bibliography

Buzan, T. (2002) *How to Mind Map*, London: Thorsons.

56

Well-formed outcomes

Helen Warner

Purpose

Problem thinking can help individuals stay stuck, so here is an easy strategy to think more positively about the outcome you would like to achieve.

Description

Think of the situation using an *outcome frame* rather than a *problem frame* as it is easier to move towards something than away from what you don't want. The outcome needs to be reasonably within your control. If it relies on the actions of others, then concentrate on how to elicit the right response.

Process

Consider the questions below:

- *What do I want?*
  - As specifically as you can. If big, break down into smaller, easier to achieve outcomes.
  - What will stop me from achieving this? This will highlight the obstacles which you need to change to outcomes.

- *How will I know when I have got it?*
  - What will you see, hear and feel? You may set a timeframe.

- *How will I start and maintain the project?*

Positive: think of what you want rather than what you don't want.

Own part: think of what you'll actively do that's within your control.

Specific: imagine the outcome as specifically as you can.

Evidence: think of the sensory-based evidence when you have got there.

Resources: do you have adequate resources/choices to get the desired outcome?

Size: is the outcome the right size?

Pitfalls

None.

Bibliography

O'Connor, J. and Seymour, J. (1990) *Introducing NLP: Psychological Skills for Understanding and Influencing People*, London: HarperCollins.

G

Relationships

57

I'm right and you're wrong

Denis Gorce-Bourge

Purpose

This strategy is really useful in a problematic relationship, either professional or personal. It requires the usual comfortable room, plus two chairs, a small table and a photo frame. The strategy will help your client get more powerful in the relationship, increasing his/her understanding of communication.

Description

This powerful strategy is a metaphor to help clients understand the relativity of truth. Two people can be talking about the same thing and have different points of view, especially when they are both looking at the same thing and seeing different realities. On the way to success, it is not rare to have communication difficulties.

I remember a difference of opinion between a human resources manager and an operations manager on what to do about a staff member. They were arguing about the right thing to do. Both had different understandings and experiences with this person. The operations manager used the strategy to help sort the problem out and find a reasonable solution, beneficial for both the staff member and the company.

Process

Your client has a problem with someone about something. It can be personal or professional. Ask your client to sit in a chair (Chair 1), opposite an empty chair (Chair 2). Chair 2 is the chair where the 'other' person is supposedly sitting. In between your client and Chair 2, you put an object, i.e. the photo frame on the small table. You decide which side the client will see from Chair 1, but it's essential that he/she sees only one side, either the picture or the back of the frame. Ask the client to describe what he/she sees from Chair 1.

After he/she does this, ask your client to go and sit on Chair 2, representing the other person in the situation, and ask your client to describe the object again from the 'other' person's perspective.

When the task is complete, ask your client to 'step out' of the situation (out of the two chairs) and tell you what he/she sees from this position. Ask the client if he/she understands the different points of view of these two people. Invite him/her to sit again in his/her chair (Chair 1) and revisit the problem. Check if your client has already changed his/her mind about the whole situation. What has he/she learned from it? If the client does not get it yet completely, ask him/her to go back to the other chair (Chair 2) and look at the situation from the other point of view. Then, seated back in Chair 1, ask the client to describe the way he/she will manage the situation now. If the person is still not clear about a new approach, start again by asking the client to describe the photo frame from each chair. If both perspectives are understood by your client, he/she will find a new way of dealing with the situation and the other person. Some clients are very quick to move on while others will need to go back and forth from Chair 1 to Chair 2 a few times to find a way to move forward, to find a new approach incorporating the other person's position and point of view.

The stronger person in a situation is the most flexible, the one able to step into the other person's shoes and to understand another perspective. To be able to use this strategy is a valuable skill to have in terms of managing relationships in the workplace.

Pitfalls

None.

58

Influencing strategy: stepping into the other person's shoes

Joan O'Connor

Purpose

This is useful when your coachee is having difficulty persuading someone to do something for them, getting agreement or acknowledgement of their point of view.

Description

In this exercise you are helping the client to influence others by seeing things from the other person's perspective.

Process

Ask the coachee to describe the person who is causing them difficulty. Ask them to describe the person's behaviours. Use the following questions as a prompt for their thinking:

- What is important to this person right now?
- What is happening in their work/life right now?
- How might this be influencing their thinking/viewpoint?
- How do they make decisions?
- How do they like to receive information?
- How does it benefit the person to agree with you/acknowledge your view?

Getting the coachee to think about the person enables them to start thinking about things from that person's perspective. If the coachee is willing it is helpful to have the coachee move to a different seat to talk about the person. The physical movement helps to create the sense of looking at things differently.

Once the coachee has explored these questions, bring them back to the issue they have, and ask them to think about how the person may see the issue and what view they may hold. Ask a question such as: 'If Jack were here now, what would he say about the issue?'. This helps the coachee see how the person might be viewing the situation, and gives them information to work with on how to approach the issue differently.

Pitfalls

Some people find it difficult to imagine what the other person is thinking. Some people don't want to think like the other person because their negative feelings are too strong. The coach may need to spend time helping the person think through the positive outcomes that he/she can achieve by being willing to think like the other person, before they will move to the specific action of doing so.

Bibliography

O'Connor, J. (2001) *NLP Workbook*, London: Thorsons.

59

The Meta Mirror

Bruce Grimley

Purpose

The purpose of the Meta Mirror model is to assist an individual to see how their difficulty in a relationship is actually a result of their relationship with themselves, rather than the relationship with the other person. It is based upon the psychodynamic concept of projection where we find other people difficult because they remind us of aspects of ourselves that we have not fully dealt with. By bringing this blind spot into conscious awareness, the Meta Mirror provides individuals with the opportunity to be more fully in control during relationships with people who have hitherto been very difficult.

Description

The Meta Mirror model was designed by Robert Dilts in 1988. Its name alludes to the psychodynamic concept of projection in that typically the people coachees have most difficulty communicating with are a mirror image of how the coachee relates to themselves in that same situation. To assist in understanding, a diagram is provided below in Figure 9 with the hypothetical labels in the text **(bold)**, visually presented.

- Ask the coachee to relate to the other person in the first position. Ask them what characteristic makes the person so difficult. Coach them to getting just the right trait, the

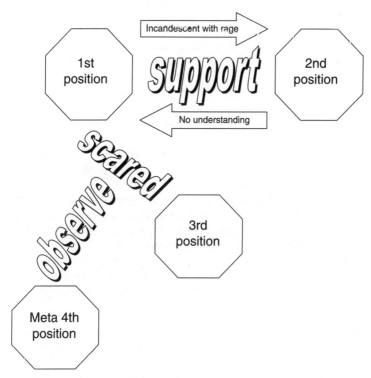

Figure 9 **The Meta Mirror in action**

one that really sums up the problem for them. **(other person has no understanding of the challenge)**

- Ask the coachee to step into the 3rd perceptual position and observe themselves in the first position. Ask them to describe themselves and then name their own behaviour in relationship to the other person. **(incandescent with rage)**
- In the 3rd perceptual position ask the coachee to raise their awareness as to how their reaction to the other person actually reinforces the relationship system, or acts as a trigger.
- Ask the coachee to think of other ways in which they could change their behaviour in this relationship.

- Ask the coachee to go into the Meta 4th position and notice how in that position they can 'see' the relationship of them in the 3rd position (fly on the wall) to them in the 1st position. Ask them to name that relationship. **(scared)** To what extent is their relationship to themselves a mirror of the other person's relationship to them in that situation?
- From the Meta 4th position ask the coachee to switch the 1st and 3rd position reactions and notice how it changes the dynamic of the relational system. Ask the coachee to now relate to the other person from this revised 1st position.
- Ask the coachee from the 2nd position, the perspective of the 'difficult person, to now observe this revised person and ask: "What does this person need from me in this situation?". Allow that person to receive this in whatever fashion they want. **(support)** Notice the change in that person from the 2nd position perspective.
- Finally, ask the coachee to re-associate into the revised 1st position. Ask the coachee to notice how this model has changed their internal experience in this relationship.

In Figure 9 we have a situation where an employee feels her line manager has no understanding of the situation they are managing; her reaction is she is incandescent with rage. When seeing herself from her 3rd perceptual position she is quite scared. She goes into the Meta 4th position and swaps the 1st and 3rd position and relates to her line manager as a scared person. On now seeing herself through her line manager's eyes she sees herself as scared and recognizes she needs to give herself support. On re-associating into her 1st position after this exercise she found her-self much more supportive of herself in this situation and her line manager no longer was a problem for her. To what extent in this situation her relationship to herself (scared) mirrored her manager's relationship to her (not having any understanding), one can only speculate.

Pitfalls

- One can get mixed up with all of the positions, so it is a good idea to mark them out on the floor and ask the other person to step into each of the spaces as one asks the questions relevant to that position.

- The material that this coaching technique uncovers often is quite unconscious. It is therefore best to just go with the answers that come to the mind of the person doing the exercise and to be pleasantly surprised, rather than analyze the answers too much.
- Allow the other person to play around with the four positions. There is no rule that says after the first run one has to come up with wonderful insight. One may need to revisit some of the positions to obtain greater clarity concerning how one really feels in that position.

Bibliography

Dilts, R. and DeLozier, J. (2000) *Encyclopedia of Systemic Neuro-Linguistic Programming and NLP New Coding*, Scotts Valley, CA: NLP University Press.

60

The Meta Mirror

Gill Hicks

Purpose

The purpose of this exercise is to help the client to be aware of relationship blindspots.

Description

What is actually communicated is what is received, not what is said. Many clients believe that what they communicate is what they say or intend. Frequently clients keep communicating to an individual in their own preferred style and are surprised and disappointed to continually get the same results! The Meta Mirror exercise is a simple, yet very powerful NLP process that can be used for any type of client – personal or business – when there are communication/relationship problems.

Process

The process involves physically changing positions. The coachee (C) sits or stands in the position they would be in if they were talking to the 'problem person' (P) and 'sees' P sitting or standing as they would if the conversation were real. C says what they want to say to P. It is very important that C then changes state – shakes off being themselves, for example by shaking arms or turning around. C then 'becomes P' – sits or stands in P's position and assumes the body language of P. In this position, they now 'hear' what C said and notice their response as P. Once again, they must change state, shaking off being P, and then move to the third position of 'Wise Advisor' where they can observe the interaction between C and P. (A few clients find it easier to stand on a chair and look down on the interaction.)

From this position as Wise Advisor, and having observed the response of P, the client as Wise Advisor can now give advice to C as to an alternative choice of words, voice, body language, etc. The client then goes back to the first position as themselves, C, and tries out the new communication to P. The process continues as many times as necessary until the response from P is satisfactory. It is very important to remind the client to change state between each position. If the client has gone round a couple of times and seems to be making little headway, you as coach will almost certainly see where the communication is falling down and may ask if you could make some suggestions in what C says or how they say it.

Example

My client Lynn was concerned about raising her professional profile within her own department. She worked very hard but was concerned that she was seen as relatively 'lightweight'. Three or four sessions into our coaching relationship, she said she was getting very frustrated by James, a senior member within her department who kept walking into her office, sitting down for up to half an hour at a time to 'bring her up to date' but mostly with information already known to Lynn. This was happening as often as twice per day, and Lynn was worried about upsetting James and indeed getting no updates if she said anything.

We used the Meta Mirror, first with Lynn's normal response when James came in. As soon as Lynn had shaken off being herself and 'became James' she realized that James had no idea that Lynn was busy and in fact assumed that Lynn welcomed James. After two rounds of the process, Lynn decided that in future she would get up from her desk and, depending on the circumstances, would alternate between being very welcoming, and saying she would love an update but was very busy at the moment – could she come and see James later? James seemed very surprised the first time Lynn used the latter response but within just a couple of days started to say: 'Is this a good time?'. We went on to use the Meta Mirror again to find a comfortable way for Lynn to interject at the start of the updates to remind James the headlines of what she already knew, saving considerable time previously used covering old ground.

Pitfalls

- Notice if the coachee refers to themselves as 'I' whilst in position P or in Wise Advisor. They should only refer to themselves C as being a third person, for example 'I think C needs to . . .'
- I would not suggest using this intervention early in a coaching relationship with a client who has difficulty getting in touch with their feelings.

Bibliography

Dilts, R. (1990) *Changing Belief Systems with NLP*, Capitola, CA: Meta Publications.

61

The Rope Game

Denis Gorce-Bourge

Purpose

You can use this strategy to help a client who is having difficulties dealing with another person in either a private or professional environment. It requires the usual comfortable setting, plus a length of rope (preferably quite a thick one), about one metre in length. The objective of the exercise is for the client to find a way to let go of the rope and let the other person deal with it.

Description

The Rope Game can help people become more aware of their responsibility and power in relationships or situations. The game uses a physical metaphor to make the obvious point that without their contribution, a problem would not exist. It gives them an opportunity to step out of the 'victim' role and allow themselves to take back control. The game also demonstrates the role the two parties play in a problematic relationship and the realization that they have power and that they can act, instead of reacting; they have power to change the situation.

Process

The Rope Game takes approximately 20 minutes and requires a metre-long piece of thick rope (so the client has something 'real' to hold on to). Ask your client to tell you about his or her problematic relationship and ask him or her to tell you how it works. Now, ask your client to hold the rope and to pull it. You now play the role of the person with whom the client has a problem. Ask your client to tell you how he/she is managing to keep the rope taut, for example arguing, being negative, etc. Explain to your client that if one of them decides not to 'play the game', then there would be no one on the other side to keep the rope taut. Keep asking your client what he/she is doing to keep the rope taut until a satisfactory explanation is given. You need the client to realise that he/she is part of the problem and can therefore be part of the solution. If he/she accepts responsibility, then he/she can act, and not be a victim any more. You are looking for the client to change his/her attitude in order to change the result that he/she is getting in the relationship.

If you are satisfied with the way the client can change the situation, with the explanation supplied, you can tell your client to take some time and when ready, to let go of the rope. Ask your client to imagine a similar situation in the future and explain how he/she feels about letting go of the rope. Can you see that your client can feel the change, feel his/her responsibility and his/her power to change the relationship? Ask your client to imagine the relationship now that the rope is no longer providing a connection between the two parties. Double check with your client and ask him or her to imagine the relationship now, with no rope connection. Letting go of the rope means accepting not being part of the problem anymore but becoming part of the solution.

Pitfalls

The pitfall in this strategy is for the coach to lose the purpose of the game. The only goal is to help the client let go of the rope or even just realize his or her involvement in the situation.

62

Understanding difference in communication/influencing styles

Penny Swinburne

Purpose

I use this exercise for looking at effectiveness in influencing and negotiating, where my client is experiencing difficulty at the relationship level, which is likely to be due to a difference in style. The model encourages people to look at their preferred style and that of others, increasing their range and flexibility of interpersonal working. It is also useful when people are working across organizational cultures, for example civil servants working with outside contractors from the private sector. It can be a real eye opener for clients to realize that some people are just different and 'different' as opposed to 'difficult' opens up ways forward.

Description

The model is based on work originally by Charles Handy. It uses three 'pure' interpersonal styles, 'Tough Battler' 'Friendly Helper' and 'Logical Thinker'. Each of us uses our own combination of the three in our communication style, particularly relevant to influencing and negotiating. The model enables us to plot ourselves and others in relation to interpersonal style and provides a way of understanding and managing differences in style, which requires no special psychometric training.

Process

The situation normally presents itself – one that your client is finding frustrating at the relationship level. Draw an equilateral triangle, with the three 'pure' styles at the corners. Give a brief explanation of the styles – the names are highly indicative.

Tough Battler

Logical Thinker   Friendly Helper

- Tough Battler – gets satisfaction from the 'fight' and competition.
- Friendly Helper – gets satisfaction from maintaining friendly relationships.
- Logical Thinker – gets satisfaction from good, clear logical arguments.

A key difference is that Tough Battler and Friendly Helper are emotionally based, whereas Logical Thinker is thinking based.

   Pull out differences in style by asking: 'How does a Tough Battler see a Friendly Helper?, etc., working through the combinations. Examples giving the flavour are:

- TB sees FH – weak, a pushover.
- FH sees TB – scary, a bully.
- LT sees FH – woolly.
- LT sees TB – illogical.
- FH sees LT – cold.
- TB sees LT – boring.

Your client then places themselves in the diagram – what mix do they see themselves as? – in the chosen situation. You can help by asking them the following questions:

- How did you go about influencing them?
- What did you say and do?
- What did you find frustrating?
- What did you find satisfying?

Your feedback on what you have heard and observed during coaching is also helpful.

The next step is to ask them to place the other person on the diagram. This in itself is often useful. Useful questions might be:

- Does the person behave in the way that frustrates you deliberately to frustrate you, or just because that's their way?
- How do they see you?
- What could you do to make your communication with that person more effective?

The last question leads to further coaching exploring strategies that your client feels could be within their range.

People understand the classification very easily, often enjoy looking at relationships this way and can get very rapid insight. Its simplicity means they can take it away and apply it to other work (and outside work) relationships.

Pitfalls

There's no simple answer! The hard work is in developing and practising other influencing strategies. Otherwise, it becomes a 'so what?' experience.

Bibliography

Handy, C. (1985) *Understanding Organizations*, London: Penguin Books.

H

Self awareness

63

A life of choice?

Aidan Tod

Purpose

This strategy helps a client to ensure they have made or are making a good career choice.

Description

We can meet clients who appear stressed and unhappy in their current role. They may be complaining of having no work/life balance. Often they express having little enthusiasm and low energy. This may indicate that they are ready for a choice point in their career. It can be helpful for the client to explore the original reasons for going into their chosen career, the strengths and capabilities they have and their hopes and dreams. The outcome of this focus is greater clarity about career choice and easier movement to action.

Process

The process starts by asking the client to think about how they chose their career. Were they influenced by family members, teachers at school? It is common to hear the client say things like 'I always wanted to be a . . .' or 'I never wanted to be a . . .' or 'My father/uncle/sister was a [xxx] and I was expected to follow'. It is helpful to focus on their feelings at different stages of their career – good and bad. Ask the client to think about what they would like to have done. Explore this and help them understand what is fuelling this idea.

What is their dream now? What would be the craziest career choice today? Encourage the client to be bold and creative. It will enable you to see where the passions and energies for this individual are. Pick up on those when you notice them and play them back to the client. Once the client has offered some alternatives it can be helpful to explore what of the current role is enjoyed now. What aspects are least enjoyed? What strengths does the individual have?

The final stage is to help the client to make some choices about actions to take. It is usual for them to have identified what it is about the current role that they are unhappy about and how they would prefer to be spending their energy. You can then help them to take some actions steps towards the role they would choose. A key for you as coach is to notice when the client's energy goes up as this is usually when they are thinking or imagining something important.

Pitfalls

None.

64

Articulating own goals, developing goal-setting strategies

Gill Dickers

Purpose

A learning contract enables course participants to use a goal-setting strategy, and to articulate and plan their own goals.

Description

Participants are encouraged to think about their goals for a training course, or programme of study and to coach each other. The framework for the session and the learning contract is based on Whitmore's (2002) GROW model. Participants are encouraged to ask open-ended questions, to listen and not advise. The session is interactive, allowing students to discuss the learning contract template and co-coach each other. It lasts about 90 minutes. Participants may focus on short-term goals (for example, time management), medium-term goals (for example, a placement proposal) or long-term goals (for example, a dissertation). The learning contract can form the basis of a future coaching discussion with a tutor or trainer. Materials required are copies of the learning contract template.

Process

Encourage the participants to use the following template, and, if this is helpful, explain the purpose of each section.

Learning contract

A Learning Contract will help you to:

- be positive about your knowledge, skills and values
- specify what your goals for learning are
- establish when and how you will achieve these
- articulate what resources and support you need to achieve your goals.

1 Goals

(a) What are my main goals for this course, or this year? *(e.g. to pass the course with an upper second, to achieve the learning outcomes, to enjoy myself)*

2 Reality

(a) What skills and strengths do I have? *(e.g. I am independent, as I travelled to India in my gap year; I am caring, as I look after my grandmother; I am bright, as I passed my degree)*

(b) What have I done and considered so far? *(e.g. I have joined the library and learned how to get web access and e-journals; I have bought a wall planner)*

3 Options

(a) What options do I have? *(e.g. get the books from the library for my first assignment; make a space to study in my house; join a sports club)*

(b) What obstacles stand in my way? *(e.g. tiredness, laziness, fear of getting things wrong)*

(c) How will I deal with these obstacles? *(e.g. make sure I eat and sleep properly; remind myself why I am here; I want to be a Vet; have a go at everything; I know I can do it)*

4 What? When? Will?

(a) What are my target dates for these long-term goals? *(e.g. an upper second degree in July 2013)*

(b)   Are there any short-term, medium-term goals on the way? *(e.g. yes, success in all my assignments)*

(c)   What support and resources do I need? *(e.g. tutors, library support staff, friends and family)*

(d)   When will I get access to these? *(e.g. plan a meeting with my tutor)*

(e)   What will I feel like when I achieve the goals? *(e.g. relieved)*

(f)   What single step will I take towards these goals? *(e.g. email my tutor and ask for a meeting)*

(g)   When will I take the steps? *(e.g. today at 4 pm)*

(h)   How committed am I, on a scale of 1–10? *(e.g. 10!)*

Signed   *Date*

Pitfalls

Some people may not respond well to being asked to plan, preferring to take a more relaxed approach to life and studies.

Bibliography

Whitmore, J. (2002) *Coaching for Performance* (2nd edition), London: Nicholas Brealey Publishing.

65

Career MOT

Diana Hogbin-Mills

Purpose

This exercise delivers prioritized insights into what motivates a client in their career and what gives them workplace satisfaction. As a result, they can clearly identify what they need to focus on to re-energize their careers. A client will gain a thorough and conscious understanding of what makes them tick, how well they are maximizing their workplace satisfaction and how they can increase it.

Description

This exercise helps a client to run an MOT on their career to find out how much energy they are leaking from their engine. The exercise surfaces emotional factors that can have a powerful impact on career decision-making. Clients probably know they exist but they're often not consciously stated or acknowledged and therefore not fully used.

Process

1 Create a template using a piece of A4 paper or bigger and turn it so that looking at it the longest edge is at the bottom. Divide the page into four by folding the page into half, then half again. This will create four columns. Add four headings, one to each column as shown in Table 2.

2 Brainstorm career motivators. Use prompts such as: 'What motivates you at work? What is important to you in the

Table 2 Career MOT template

Motivator	Opportunity	Threat	Opportunity cost

world of work? Add responses to the Motivator column. Example responses are challenging work, interesting people, money and flexible working hours. Try for 10 motivators. Ask clients to assign 100 points across all motivators to create a prioritized list (see example below). Put numbers in brackets next to motivators.

3 Ask: 'How easy is it to satisfy these career motivators in your current situation?'. Assign a value to the Opportunity column, where 1 = not at all easy; 5 = somewhat easy; and 10 = very easy. Discuss how they arrived at the scores (for example, ask: 'What makes achieving a motivator easy for you?') and add any notes to the Opportunity column.

4 Ask: 'What is the impact on your work performance of not satisfying this motivator?'. Assign a value to the Threat column, where 1 = small; 5 = medium; and 10 = big.

5 Add notes in the Threat column as to how it impacts their performance.

6 Calculate the Opportunity Cost: multiply the scores in the Motivator, Opportunity and Threats columns. Identify the three highest Opportunity Cost scores, indicating where essential repair is most needed and can be readily achieved. Check to see whether they are what the client wants to work on and identify actions for each score that they want to address. Identify what they can do in the short, medium and long term. Look also at the Threat column for any large scores that have not already been addressed, discuss possible actions that can be planned.

Table 3 (see over) presents on example of the above.

Table 3 Career MOT template: example

Motivator	Opportunity	Threat	Opportunity Cost
Challenges (30)	10 – just need to ask	5 – lose motivation if not part of job	1,500
Money (30)	1 – I have been told there is no budget for pay rises	10 – currently don't feel valued	300
etc.			

Pitfalls

A client may not want to go through the discipline of thinking through what is important to them on a personal level and how they can proactively increase their chances for work satisfaction.

Bibliography

Ali, L. and Graham, B. (1996) *The Counselling Approach to Careers Guidance*, London: Routledge.

66

Career reputation

Diana Hogbin-Mills

Purpose

This exercise provides a clear understanding about what a client needs to do. It builds a reputation that will gain them the profile they seek. It provides the client with a clear understanding of what their career influencers think about them and, if necessary, what they need to do to change their perceptions.

Description

Use this exercise if a client has stalled in their career, been turned down for a new role, does not know how well they are performing or they want to know how they can get on. The exercise will provide invaluable insight into what is stopping them from progressing forward in their chosen direction.

Process

1 Set the scene by describing the following situations:

- Scenario 1 – Two people are sitting at their desks talking together quietly.
- Scenario 2 – A colleague is sitting at their desk at 9am, reading a newspaper.

If you ask the client to describe the people/situations, typical responses you may get are as follows:

- Scenario 1 – gossiping, considerate about the people around them, depends on what they are talking about.
- Scenario 2 – lazy, came in early so having a break, depends on what they are reading, etc.

The point of the above exercise is to highlight just how quickly we make judgements of people, either positive or negative.

2 Ask the client: 'Do the people who can influence your career have the right impression of you? Have they seen you in the light you want to be seen in?'.

3 Brainstorm a possible set of skills/behaviours (up to seven) that the client wants to be known for. These should be those that will help them in their career development that they currently demonstrate or could demonstrate. (Refer them to their company's competency framework, their current/ desired job role and their manager for valued skills/behaviours). In this exercise, the client should ideally be looking for skills/behaviours that are/can be made a strength.

4 Ask the client to identify up to five people to give them feedback. These should not be their friends and they may be either well known to them or not, but they must have an influence on their career. Ask the client if you can send out the list of skills/behaviours to the feedback providers asking them to evaluate the client. In this way you will be encouraging honest responses with the understanding that the feedback will be discussed with the client as part of their development. Devise a rating scale to evaluate the client against their skills/values. Example rating scales are: 1 to 5 where 1 = demonstrates regularly and 5 = not at all; role model, work still needed, not known for. Add in a 'Don't know' category as this in itself is telling and the client needs to work on making sure that their feedback providers are aware of what they do. Invite the feedback providers to add comments to each skill/behaviour they rate, explaining their score. Ask the client to rate their performance on their skills/behaviours and compare this with the feedback providers. Also, ask if there are skills that they want/expect them to demonstrate if they were to

see the client achieving the career development goal they have set. Table 4 presents a worked example.

5 When you have the feedback, look at the differences between what your client says and what their feedback providers say. The differences in opinions are where there nuggets of gold lie. This signals where work on changing perception will have the biggest impact on reputation.

6 Support the client to hold feedback conversations. For example, draft conversation starters with the feedback providers to identify and agree specific actions they need to take in order to change their perceptions.

7 Review actions that the client needs to take as a result of the conversations. If they need to get better at a skill/ behaviour then they can use the next exercise to role model people who are perceived to do it well.

Pitfalls

A client may not want to ask for feedback from their colleagues.

Table 4 Career reputation exercise

Skills/behaviours	Client rating	Feedback ratings	Comments
Positively influencing peers on joint projects	4	Don't know	I have not seen evidence of this to be able to comment – manager
		1	Jo is great at influencing how we spend our time on projects we work on, especially when we have tight deadlines – co-worker
Time management for monthly progress reporting on financials	2	4	Jo can sometimes leave the report creation until the last minute and seems to spend too much time worrying about reconciling pennies when I am just interested in the big numbers – manager

Bibliography

Hodgson, S. (2005) *Finding Square Holes: Discover Who You Really Are and Find the Perfect Career*, Carmarthen: Crown House Publishing.

67

Coaching glass ceiling clients

Darryl Stevens

Purpose

A number of my senior coaching clients have wanted help
to progress their career to the next elite level. Their leadership style and developed capabilities have served them well
until now, but something is missing and hindering their
progress.

Description

The aim of this coaching strategy is for the client to look
through the metaphoric glass ceiling and identify how to
break through it. There are three components, as explained
below.

Process

Looking through the glass ceiling

Your client's thoughts on their next steps need to be explored,
stretched and crystallized. Clarity on the purpose of their
ambition is also important to identify. With eyes open or
closed, ask them to consider the furthest position on a relevant time line (for example, three years) and invite them to
tell you about their lifestyle, family and health, with a particular focus on the components of their job. It is important
that they use present-tense language so that they are talking
as if they were living that life right now. Invite them to

express how they are feeling, comment on their presence, verbal and non-verbal communication and challenge them on the extent to which their purpose is being fulfilled. Equally, encourage and reinforce their conviction to succeed as they move into a place of experiential realization.

Repeat the technique as you progress back along the time line towards the present day, integrating a Gestalt approach by inviting the client to change seats for the different years explored, powerfully experiencing what success would feel like. Capture the plan on paper using a straight line to represent the period of time explored. Recording actions and achievements on opposite sides of the line, this Meaningful Action Plan with Purpose (MAPP) will enable positive movement through the glass ceiling.

Tools and capabilities

Using a positive psychology approach, identify what has served the executive in achieving their success to date. Then ask, 'What else do you need?'. Feedback from their manager and peers would be useful here. You may identify some missing elements yourself as the coaching relationship develops, for example, an opportunity to enhance their communication style, their drive to win, an action orientation. The overall outcome of this conversation should awaken their spirit, reignite their ambition and sharpen their tools to break through the glass ceiling.

Current and future systems

Invite your client to review the components of their corporate environment, for example, company culture, their manager, decision makers, opportunities, along with the environment they wish to progress into. Clients often comment on the value of this exploration to achieve an enhanced understanding of how they need to shift in order to progress. Their immediate line manager is also an important factor as they could be your client's best sponsor or indeed blocker. Ask if their manager knows about their desire to progress; are they supportive, threatened, fearful of losing them? Does the client aspire to their manager's role? Their responses will aid the client to identify meaningful choices in positively influencing the system of which they are a key part.

Pitfalls

Look out for superficial plans, thoughts and a non-committal wish list. Tone of language, energy and body language will provide any signals to pick up on and challenge. Enquire into their willingness to change and also their purpose in wanting to progress. These deep-rooted questions and the holistic approach detailed above will assist your client to break through their glass ceiling and realize their ambitions.

68

Coordinated management of meaning

Elspeth Campbell

Purpose

This strategy enables a person's resilient and independent choice making about what to do next when their feeling response is strong enough to cloud their judgement. Bringing to conscious awareness the pattern of feeling, thought and action creates the potential to reshape that pattern. It can be used at any moment in the coaching when the coach notices a repetition of expression of strong feeling emanating from the coachee and the coach hypothesizes that some exploration would assist both to be released from the grip of this emotion. Once released it will show in the coachee coming across to others in more appropriate ways. Looking through a magnifying glass in this way at a replay of an emotionally significant interaction which the coachee has been in can help to create a transformational shift into a new and more useful pattern of feeling, thought and action. This brings an immediate fine tuning of the impact s/he has on others and a commitment to try and mentally step back and reflect, before reacting, when an overwhelming feeling response happens in future.

Description

Many people can respond to strong emotion by reacting in an extreme way. When this happens, careful thought is overwhelmed by the internal feeling experience and by injunctions we have created, in the form of scripts and stories. These scripts and stories are belief systems that guide our actions and in coordinated management of meaning (CMM) theory these are referred to as contexts.

In any human interaction we create practised patterns of feeling, thought and action that become habitual; mostly we are not fully conscious of them. CMM – a theory of communication – helps us understand that these patterns are coordinated around the meanings we give to them and these meanings are embedded within our belief systems. So in order to change these patterns, which, having become habitual, are rather ingrained, it is our belief systems that require shifting. This can happen when we bring to consciousness the patterns and the beliefs that shape them. We become able to exercise choice, rather than simply react, about how the pattern is connected together. For example, once a belief system has shifted, with the same emotion a different thought may be generated, or with the same emotion and thought a different action may be generated.

Within CMM the contexts containing belief systems are named as follows:

- socio-economic stories
- family scripts
- personal identity stories
- organizational culture stories
- professional scripts
- managerial scripts
- relational stories.

Process

Become attuned to the feelings expressed by the coachee in their talk, in the way they come across and in the feelings and images you have yourself that could be an expression of their emotion. Invite the coachee to explore the emotional content that is coming in to the coaching space by naming it and explaining, tentatively, how you see it may be impacting other things the coachee wants to achieve. Once your invitation to explore is accepted, begin to facilitate a collaborative exploration of an episode of the coachee in interaction in the following way:

1 **Utterance** – identify a word or phrase with accompanying emotional content that has made you curious, usually by the force or tone with which this is expressed, or by repetition.

2 **Critical incident** – let unfold a detailed description of the episode of interaction, and ask:

- Who said what?
- Who responded and how?
- What happened next?

3 **Feeling and bodily response** – name the emotion expressed by the coachee and ask:

- What would you call this feeling?
- What did you notice in yourself at a non-verbal level? How did your body react?
- What did you notice about the other person's/people's body language?

4 **Thought (i.e. meaning)** – discover together the meaning that the coachee attributes to his/her feeling and bodily response by asking:

- How did you interpret what you felt?
- Is there another time where you remember the same feeling and what did it mean then?
- Are there other possible interpretations for what it means now?

5 **Choice of action** – explore what happened next by asking:

- What did you do?
- How did your feeling and your interpretation affect the way you acted?

As you go through this process, you will hear the coachee express the stories and scripts that guided his/her action. This will help you develop a hypothesis about the beliefs within the contexts that are guiding the pattern of feeling, thought and action. Share this developing hypothesis with the coachee, offering it in a tentative way to encourage a dialogue so that the coachee begins to voice ideas about how the pattern could be different, in a process of self-discovery.

Pitfalls

For you to work in this way, a capacity for reflexivity is required, which is the ability to act as an observer to oneself in interaction with another person and, in so doing, to discover and be informed by the response one is creating in others by one's actions. Without this self awareness it would be difficult to analyze the coachee's way of being. Using your capacity for reflexivity slows you down to a point of calm analysis, which helps you discern the minute and subtle detail of the way the pattern is constructed.

Bibliography

Cronen, V. E. (1992) 'Coordinated management of meaning: theory for the complexity and contradictions of everyday life'. (pp. 183–207), in Siegfried, J. (ed) *The Status of Common Sense in Psychology*, Norwood, NJ: Ablex.
Oliver, C. (2005). *Reflexive Inquiry*, London: Karnac Books.

69

Developing independent skills

Gill Dickers

Purpose

When starting a new course or training programme, participants may feel both excited and apprehensive. This exercise always helps people meet and talk to each other, and it builds confidence. It encourages participation and learning.

Description

A 'hopes, fears and resolution' workshop for groups of up to 24 encourages participants to explore their feelings about being on a training programme, enables interaction and promotes group building. By using drawing, discussion and music, students with different learning styles have the opportunity to develop supportive networks and build their confidence. It takes about 90 minutes. It is better to leave more time than to rush the session. Materials required are flip chart paper, blue tack, felt tips and quiet music.

Process

I have identified five steps for the strategy:

1 *Introduction and rules:* As part of the exercise, group boundaries need to be agreed. Examples are: participants should listen and respect each others' views, and keep all information confidential.
2 *Initial meeting and group building, with quiet music:*

Participants select a partner who they don't know. One is 'A' and one is 'B'. They tell each other three light-hearted things about themselves: this may be about their hobbies, family or a recent holiday. They each introduce their new partner to another pair, the 'A's introduce the 'B's' and vice versa. This group of four then divides a flip chart sheet into three, possibly using the template of a shield or heart, and labels the sections 'hopes', 'fears' and 'resolutions'. They write or draw their thoughts and feelings about the course.

3 *More group developments:* The groups of four join another group of four, introduce each other and discuss what they have included on their flip charts. Discussion topics could be about similarities and differences between the groups, how they could meet their hopes for the course, and how their fears could be resolved.

4 *Review and evaluation:* The flip charts are stuck to the wall and the leader draws out the themes, taking care to give information and support to the students. Towards the end of the session, the leader asks participants to say what has gone well in the session and what has not gone well.

5 *Reflection and endings:* Each member of the group privately records their observations about the workshop and what they have noticed about themselves. The leader should give positive feedback to the group and thank them for their participation.

Pitfalls

Be prepared for the 'fears' and have information at hand to resolve these as much as is possible.

70

Feed back or fight back

Denis Gorce-Bourge

Purpose

The way we talk to people sometimes produces unexpected results. We can be totally unaware that our speaking manner is aggressive, our tone judgemental, our comments dismissive or our feedback condescending. Usually, a person's reaction will give us a clue as to how feedback is received. Sometimes though, the person delivering the feedback can react as if they are the victim. This may result in a complete misunderstanding and a potentially significant conflict.

This strategy is designed for professional or personal situations where the client is getting a result that is very different from what he/she anticipates. Its purpose is to make the client aware of the cause and effect that they are producing. A conflictual situation between two people is the result of both their attitudes towards each other. As they say, 'it takes two to tango'.

Description

This strategy can help the client learn more about their attitude and behaviour towards others. It will help them avoid starting a 'fire' when all they really want to do is help. This strategy will help the client understand that the way we communicate is a powerful tool, but most of the time we are not aware of the power it has, and instead get dragged down into painful conflictual situations. The main objective of the strategy is for the client to stop the psychological games and become responsible for what they get from others as human beings, executives, fathers, husbands.

Process

Put two chairs in front of each other. For ease of understanding, your client will be A and the other person in the situation will be B. Ask A to sit in a chair and to tell you about the situation with B, then about his/her feelings, what he/she feels about the situation or the person. You should at this stage have an idea of what the problem is, for example frustration, anger or jealousy. Once the game is uncovered, the client can be coached to find alternative strategies.

Pitfalls

There are no major pitfalls in this strategy. For the person using the strategy, it is just about helping the client to visit the other point of view in order to understand reaction and in the future to be able to act according to the goal to get the right result.

71

Finding what makes you tick at work

Anne Archer

Purpose

Sometimes a client needs some help working out what it is they do when they are at their best. This can also be referred to as being in flow. The benefits for understanding this are numerous and include making better job choices, understanding what motivates staff, knowing what situations someone needs to sell themselves in and knowing why a job isn't working. What is important with this exercise is that it focuses on when a person is at their best. There is no room for what does not work for them.

Description

In this exercise, what you are eliciting from the client are some examples of where they have achieved in life. You explore the details before identifying patterns and themes. It is important to note that this exercise is about identifying success stories, not where it could have gone better.

Process

Step 1 is to generate multiple situations over the individual's life that have been rewarding and where they have felt good. A good way of helping this along is by drawing a line across a piece of paper marked off to represent years of a person's life or decades – depending on age! Thinking about achievements in specific time periods often generates less obvious ones. If there are periods of time where few achievements occur, that too is useful data later.

Step 2 is delving in a bit deeper to each achievement by finding out what happened:

- How did you get involved?
- What drew you to do this particular thing?
- As you went about [xxx], what did you do?
- How did you keep going?
- Who else was involved?
- What impact did you have on each other?
- What feedback did you get?
- How did you know it went well?
- What did you feel when it finished?
- Which bits do you retain/want to retain?
- What makes it an achievement in your eyes?

Step 3 is about looking for patterns and themes that keep occurring:

- What do you and your client notice?
- Which periods of time had more examples?
- What does this mean to you now?

Look out for whether certain types of people keep appearing. Maybe the individual is at their best under pressure or working to really tight deadlines. Perhaps working on their own is important to them, or being in a good strong team. What kinds of work is the individual doing when they are at their best? It could be that having a healthy balance between work and home is really important.

Step 4 uses the information to make plans for the future. The question to be answered is: So what? What can you do with this information? Knowing what the conditions are to be at one's best is critical. Then the secret is to work out how to create those conditions more often and so increase the chances of replicating when at one's best.

Pitfalls

It can take some people a while to think they have achieved anything. They don't have to be huge world-changing events. Patterns and themes can come from lots of smaller examples.

Bibliography

Isbister, N. and Robinson, M. (1999) *Who do you Think you Are?*, London: HarperCollins.

72

Force field analysis for organizations and individuals in transition

Christine K. Champion

Purpose

Force field analysis was developed by Lewin (1951) and is widely used to inform decision-making, particularly in planning and implementing change management programmes in organizations. It is also a useful tool for self-analysis. It is a powerful method for gaining a comprehensive overview of the different forces acting on a potential issue, and for assessing the source and strength of these. The driving and restraining forces should be sorted around common themes and should then be scored according to their 'magnitude', ranging from 1 (weak) to 10 (strong). The score may well not balance on either side, resulting in non-equilibrium.

Description

To drive change effectively:

- First, an organization has to unfreeze the driving and restraining forces that hold it in a state of quasi-equilibrium.
- Second, an imbalance is introduced to the forces to enable the change to take place. This can be achieved by increasing the drivers, reducing the restraints or both.
- Third, once the change is complete, the forces are brought back into quasi-equilibrium and re-frozen.

Process

The coach works with the client in the following way:

- Describe the current situation as it is now and the desired situation as the vision for the future.
- Identify what will happen if there is no action taken.
- List all the driving and restraining forces for the change.
- Discuss the key restraining forces and determine their strength.
- Discuss the key driving forces and determine their strength.
- Allocate a score to each using a numerical scale where 1 is very weak and 10 is very strong.
- Chart the forces by listing, in strength scale, the driving forces on the left and the restraining forces on the right.
- Explore the restraining forces and the best way to address them.
- Explore the driving forces and the best way of advancing them.
- Identify priorities and produce an action plan
- Some types of forces to consider:
  - available resources
  - traditions
  - vested interests
  - organizational structures
  - relationships
  - social or organizational trends
  - attitudes of people
  - regulations
  - personal or group needs
  - present or past practices
  - institutional policies or norms
  - agencies
  - values
  - desires
  - costs
  - people
  - events.

Pitfalls

None.

Bibliography

Lewin, K. (1951) *Field Theory in Social Science*, London: Tavistock.

73

Foxy/donkey guide to organizational politics

Helen Warner

Purpose

For many, an organization's politics are to be avoided or the
benefits are misunderstood. Typically, the area is described
in negative terms, but using this strategy can reframe it
and the individual can identify the potential benefits for
both themselves and the organization if they engage with
integrity.

Description

This model has two dimensions relating, first, to the skills of
'reading' the politics of an organization and, second, to the
skills or behaviours an individual brings to these situations
that may predispose them to either act with integrity or play
psychological games.

Process

In this exercise, help the individual to work out where they
are on the model presented in Figure 10 by just showing the
axis and four blank quadrants. Such is the closeness of these
behaviours that it is not unusual for an individual to put
themselves between two or more quadrants. Then explain
the matrix in more detail. Do they recognize the animals?
Do they sometimes move into the fox or donkey quadrants?
Can they identify an owl who could be a good role model?

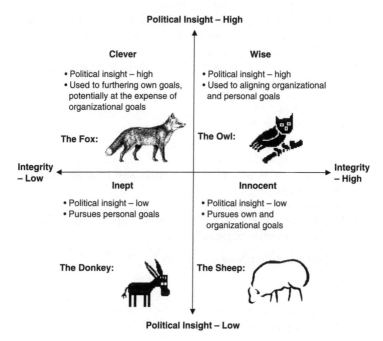

Political Insight – High

Clever
- Political insight – high
- Used to furthering own goals, potentially at the expense of organizational goals

The Fox:

Wise
- Political insight – high
- Used to aligning organizational and personal goals

The Owl:

Integrity – Low

Integrity – High

Inept
- Political insight – low
- Pursues personal goals

The Donkey:

Innocent
- Political insight – low
- Pursues own and organizational goals

The Sheep:

Political Insight – Low

Figure 10 **Organization politics exercise**

Identify the 'wise' behaviours

The good news is that constructive and positive behaviours can be learned. Behaviours and strategies to develop include:

1 Influence

- Form 'win-win' alliances with others by aligning goals and demonstrating how a strategy can be mutually advantageous.
- Work with other internal resources to maximise the effectiveness of a business area.

2 Building relationships

- Do not make assumptions about how others may be thinking or feeling. Ask open questions to understand issues from another person's perspective.

- Create a climate of trust – be open yourself by expressing your own views and beliefs, which will encourage
  others to be open and honest.
- Demonstrate active listening by checking and summarizing what you've heard.

3 Being seen and heard
   Factors to be seen

- Create a profile and get your face known.
- 'Manage by walking about'.
- Give advice or an opinion in response to a request for
  information.
- Get your name known.
- Volunteer for extra projects that are cross-
  organizationally oriented.

   Factors to be heard

- Respect.
- Trust.
- Knowledge credibility.
- Clarity of message.
- Confidence.

These strategies not only equip individuals to operate with
integrity and pursue their own and the organization's goals,
but will also address one of the key corporate challenges of
developing highly effective teams.

Bibliography

Baddeley, S. and James, K. (1987) 'Owl, fox, donkey or sheep: political skills for managers', *Management Learning*, 18(1): 3–19.

74

From manager to leader – the transition struggle

Darryl Stevens

Purpose

Executives who are promoted to senior ranks early in their career can find themselves leading a business and a large team without true leadership experience. They have moved from manager to leader and need to discover their authentic leadership style, fast.

Description

Three development dimensions can accelerate this shift, as shown in Figure 11. The strategy is adapted from research by Professor Herminia Ibarra, the Insead Chaired Professor of Organizational Behaviour.

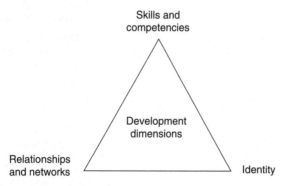

Figure 11 **Development dimensions**

Process

Skills and competencies

Ask your client to identify the skills and competencies that a top leader needs to have, calling upon three great leaders who they admire to talk about their style, skills, what they do and how they do it. Summarize their thoughts on paper and review the list together, challenging for clarity and to reveal gaps, while also reinforcing positive identifications.

Ask the executive to score themself on a scale of 1–5 against each skill noted (5 being fully competent) and then prioritize in order of importance for the leadership role they are fulfilling. Their desired future score should then be stated against each leadership competency, which will enable a discussion on the actions that are required to close the gap between the current and desired rating (see Table 5). It will become clear that using old skills alone is not enough to fulfill their new role.

Table 5 Identifying developmental actions

Priority	Skill	Current level (1–5)	Desired level (1–5)	Actions
1	Strategic planning	3	4	• Understand corporate vision • Set departmental vision and goals
2	Team engagement	2	5	• Regular two-way communication • Reward and recognition
3	Delegating	2	4	• Handover tactical tasks • Make the team accountable

Relationships and networks

Strong networking and relationship skills differentiate a good manager from a great leader. With the purpose, vision and goals of the business/department known, invite your client to think strategically as to whom they need to be in contact with. Capture this information in a spider diagram and then repeat the exercise from a tactical stance using a different coloured pen.

The next stage is to identify which groups and individuals are already established as part of the client's network and which are not. Previous networks may still be relevant but there will most certainly be a need to expand. Ask how the client has established good relationships and networks previously, what works for them, how they have perhaps been 'networked' and how they received this. Using the learning from this strengths-based approach, agree upon a time-bound action plan.

Identity

How does your client want to be perceived as a leader and how do they want to adapt their identity for different stakeholders? Using chairs in the room to represent each stakeholder (for example, staff, the managing board, customers) invite your client to sit in the place of the stakeholder and to provide the ideal feedback that this group or individual would give on your client's identity and reputation. As they experience the role of the stakeholder, comment on their delivery, focusing on their verbal and body language, since they will be displaying characteristics of the identity they wish to create. Your feedback will re-enforce these behaviours as those to be lived back in the 'real world'.

Pitfalls

As an established manager promoted to a leadership role, the auto-reflex will be to do what they have done before. Be robust and stimulating as the coach, since sustainable change needs to be provoked deep down. Asking 'Who are you, who do you need to become and how do you want to develop?' will encourage change to take place at the core of their being. Integrating this approach with action-oriented coaching will put your client on the fast track to an effective transition.

75

Identifying work-based skills

Penny Swinburne

Purpose

People often have difficulty knowing the skills they use in their work – they take what they do well for granted. This is a problem when they need to sell their skills to others, for example in appraisals or job interviews. This exercise helps to raise the client's awareness of their skills and provides them with a 'skills vocabulary'. If relevant, the skills can then be looked at to identify 'transferable skills' – those that could apply in a different role. Additionally, it builds confidence in what the client does well, particularly useful if the need for the audit is an enforced job change, or where confidence has been knocked.

Description

The client describes something they do well at work. The coach, through questioning and feedback, elicits the skills used to achieve this. This passes on the technique to the client, who can repeat it, perhaps with friends/colleagues, with other relevant activities from current and/or past jobs, to give a full skills audit. This can be checked out at a further coaching session.

Process

Start by asking the client to identify something in their work experience that they feel they did particularly well or consider an achievement. Write this up in the centre of a flip chart. Your role is then to ask questions and give feedback on the skills you can see. Useful questions/feedback includes:

* What exactly did you do?
* Tell me more about that.
* How do you know you did it well?
* So that means you . . . [e.g. were good at getting agreement between people with very different backgrounds]?
* It sounds as if you were . . . [e.g. using meeting deadline skills there]?

The coach writes up skills and evidence as they emerge, creating a 'spider' diagram. Alternatively, it can be recorded as: 'What I did' on the left hand side of the page; and 'Skills' and 'Evidence' (as in 'how do you know you did it well') on the top and bottom halves of the right hand side of the page. This can be repeated with other achievements if there is time.

Your key role is to constantly feedback positive outcomes, the skills you see that helped to accomplish this, creating positive energy and taking the client beyond 'this is what I did'. Either you or your client can write. Many clients find it difficult to think at this level and write at the same time, so it may be more helpful if you do.

The main purpose is to pass on a way of thinking to your client, so that they can then do a more thorough skills audit, maybe with the support of friends/colleagues, going over any of their past/present jobs that may be relevant. Structured paper work for this with headings for each chosen task – 'What exactly did you do?, "How do you know you did it well?", "What skills did you use?" – can be useful.

Pitfalls

Some people have real difficulty applying the word 'skill' to anything that is not really exceptional. It helps then to avoid words like 'achievement' and to find words that they can accept.

76

Improving performance by accessing emotions

Aidan Tod

Purpose

This approach is useful with people who believe that emotions have no place at work. They may not be able to access their own emotions or sometimes those of others there. The aim is to highlight how emotions affect our decision making and behaviour all the time, whether we are conscious of it or not.

Description

There are still clients who do not acknowledge that emotions have a healthy role to play in everyday working life. Often these are people who have limiting beliefs, which prevent them from accessing these powerful feelings. This exercise is designed to ameliorate this situation.

Process

The starting point arrives when a client says something to indicate that emotions shouldn't feature in the workplace, or only refers to what they think, never acknowledging their feelings in any given situation. Consider with the client a range of situations where feelings affect decision making, for example, a heated pricing discussion with a customer, appraisal rounds or wanting to promote someone and you are told you cannot. It might be that a decision needs to be taken and the logical, rational approach is not coming up with an answer that feels right. Your role is to highlight how everyone has emotions and how to be aware of them so that you can know what they are telling you and therefore make more informed choices and better decisions both in regard to self and others.

Pitfalls

None really. People have different levels of ability to get in touch with what they are feeling – but even awareness of tension and what causes it is helpful.

77

Journal writing

Caroline Shola Arewa

Words are a form of Action capable of influencing Change.
(Ingrid Bengis)

Purpose

This strategy uses words and creativity to support clients
as they learn and change as a result of coaching. Most
change occurs between sessions and it's good to have ways of
processing insights as they arise.

Description

Journaling works with the unconscious mind as it processes
data from the conscious mind. This journaling technique
offers a series of questions that can be used as they are, or
adapted by clients to record their inner journey of change.

Early in the coaching relationship the client can be
invited to keep a journal. It acts as a companion throughout
the coaching journey, detailing achievements, progress, obstacles, weaknesses, insights and successes. Clients can then
see at a glance how they are developing. It can be done any way
the client chooses. This exercise is offered as a starting place.

Process

A journal is an excellent tool for enhancing performance and
success levels. It allows you to express creativity and also

keep a record of your achievements and plans. Most of us keep notes and diaries but journaling is *writing on purpose*. Keeping a journal helps put words into action and change dreams into reality. It can help clarify, organize and reveal hidden parts of yourself and propel you towards greater achievement on all levels. Remember, your journal is personal; only share it if you wish to.

When writing, let the words flow; don't be concerned about grammar or prose. Try not to stand in judgement of yourself; there is no right or wrong way to keep a personal journal. Let the free spontaneous process of writing be a tool to work through conflicts. Witness your ideas becoming organized. It's wonderful to write after meditation as it allows you to capture any Aha moments, where all of a sudden everything makes sense. As you reflect on your journal it will reveal what you most need to know about yourself. Everything is a valuable part of your journey.

You will require a large A4, lined or unlined journal/notebook, pens and willingness to write freely and uncensored. Use the exercise below as a guide.

Daily journal suggested questions

Answer the following questions or others daily to enhance success:

- How did I spend my alone time today?
- How well did I communicate with people today?
- What can I improve?
- What was my biggest lesson today?
- What am I most grateful for today?
- How have I moved towards greater success?
- How much have I invested in my health today?
- What did I do really well today?
- What are my priorities for tomorrow?

Pitfalls

There are no associated problems with journaling when used in a coaching context. The client remains in control; however, this exercise sometimes uncovers difficult emotions.

Bibliography

Arewa, C. S. (2003) *Embracing Purpose, Passion and Peace*, London: Inner Vision Books.

78

Noticing and paying attention to metaphors

Angela Dunbar

Purpose

This is a strategy to help you and your clients become more aware of how the everyday metaphors they use may be shaping their thoughts. By paying attention to metaphors and asking questions about them, clients gain understanding about their situation and how they are thinking about it from a very different perspective. The exercise is a really useful way to explore difficult or sensitive issues, as the client can describe the metaphors in detail without needing to worry about explaining the 'real situation' to you. It can also be time saving.

Description

People use metaphors all the time to describe how they feel and what they want. You may just think of metaphor as simply a creative way to impart a message, but many linguists and psychologists believe now that they are far more than this. In fact, a metaphoric description may be a closer representation of what's really going on in our minds, as highlighted by George Lakoff and Mark Johnson (1980) in their book *Metaphors We Live By*: 'the human conceptual system is metaphorically structured and defined . . .' (p. 6).

Metaphors are being expressed constantly as a way of describing our thinking patterns all the time – Penny Tompkins and James Lawley (2006) suggest that the average person uses several metaphors in every minute of conversation. And that doesn't tell us how many unexpressed metaphors may be 'just outside' the person's awareness, but be part of their thought processes. Many facilitators and coaches are discovering that Clean Language can have extraordinary results. This is a questioning process created by New Zealand psychotherapist David Grove, which enables clients to go deeper into their own thoughts, habits and perceptions, where they can find their own unique solutions. The 'deepness' of thinking is enhanced by asking clean questions of the metaphoric content of the client's language. This focuses their attention on the *structure* of their thinking and experience, rather than the same old problem-content that they've thought in the same old way many times before. This enables a different level of thinking, leading to different kinds of creative solutions. To paraphrase Einstein's thoughts on creativity: *no problem can be solved from the same level of consciousness that created it.*

Process

Rather than plan to use this as a stand-alone exercise, just begin to notice how often the client gives you metaphoric descriptions of their situation and what they'd like to do about it. Here are some examples you are very likely to hear:

- 'I feel like I'm banging my head against a brick wall.'
- 'She's closed herself off from me and I don't know how to break through.'
- 'I need a bit of a jump-start.'

When you notice a metaphor, ask a few simple Clean Language questions to have the client become more aware of their metaphoric thinking. When using Clean Language in this way, generally you want to repeat back the metaphoric words to the client exactly as they used them: 'You're off balance today. What kind of "off balance" is that "off balance"?'. Make a note of whatever the client says next and again repeat back their words.

Then ask: 'And when you are feeling "off balance", is there anything else about feeling off balance?'. Continue to explore whatever the client says, paying particular attention to the metaphoric language they use. Repeat back the client's words and use these two questions only: *'What kind of [xxxx] is that [xxxx]?'* and *'And is there anything else about that [xxxx]?'*. The idea here is to have the client become aware of something about their pattern of thinking that they weren't aware of before. Metaphorically, the exercise is like holding a mirror up to the client, and everything you say is reflecting back to the client their own pattern of thinking.

If the client starts to go a bit 'dreamy' and seems deep in their own thoughts, the chances are they are accessing deep stuff and probably gaining some new insights. This example process has no 'formal' beginning, ending or time limit. You can use it as and when appropriate. You may choose to move on to another kind of questioning or continue with another Clean Language process or exercise (see the other strategies in this book).

Pitfalls

Some people don't use metaphors so frequently. It doesn't mean that they don't think in this way, just that they may not be able to consciously access these thoughts too easily. So, typically when you ask questions of any metaphors these kinds of people do use, they'll give you lots of conceptual descriptions rather than develop their metaphor. If this is the case, work with them on whatever comes up, even if there are no metaphors. Bide your time and when they do give a metaphor, be patient when exploring it. These kinds of people, when they do 'get into' their metaphors, often find it immensely rewarding as it really gives them insights at a very different level to their normal conscious thinking.

Bibliography

Grove, D. and Panzer, B. (1989) *Resolving Traumatic Memories: Metaphors and Symbols in Psychotherapy*, New York, NY: Irvington.

Lakoff, G. and Johnson, M. (1980) *Metaphors We Live By*, Chicago, IL: University of Chicago Press.

Tompkins, P. and Lawley, J. (2006) *Coaching with Metaphor*, first published in *Cutting Edge Coaching Techniques Handbook*, London: CIPD Coaching At Work.

79

People will not change unless they want to – so locate the desire to change first

Peter Melrose

Purpose

Often we approach change by setting goals, reviewing options, agreeing and implementing plans. But the will to act is tacitly assumed – and it is not always there. This strategy is about helping your client find the desire to change. It is *the* vital step, for example where an organization wants your client to change but the client does not, stuck in an assumption that the 'problem' is not their own, but the organization's.

Description

This strategy focuses on the challenges of change. In particular, it encourages the client to clearly identify their desire for change and the current reality.

Process

The change equation ($D \times V \times P = C$) is a very useful explanation of the challenge of change for individuals. D is the personal *desire* to change or the level of *dissatisfaction* with how things are; V is a clear personal *vision* of how it will be like for the individual, once change is achieved; and P are the *practical steps* necessary to take to make change happen. C equals the *cost of achieving change* successfully and the equation is saying that D, V and P all need to be in place to outweigh the perceived cost to the individual of making change.

So, do not let the initial coaching objectives (which reflect your client's conscious concerns) constrain the process too much. These are likely to change in time. Work by following the energy of your client in how they are making sense of the world around them. Allow the client to express feelings of frustration and uncertainty from an empathic place. The challenge, though, is continually to relate back to where the client is and where they feel they want to be, to keep them focused on their personal choices to think, to feel and to act.

Probe the value to your client of the perception of others in the organization as opposed to the objectivity of data: explore the view that perception is reality and that people's feelings are valid data too. Ask what it would be like if they did see a need for change. Ask what is likely to happen if they do not.

When you are making some progress around the client's engagement with change, explore the change equation together. Keep under review yourself the extent to which the client accepts the need for change; and what change exactly. Do not necessarily ask the direct question 'Are you up for change?' because it is not likely to elicit useful data.

If necessary, challenge the client directly about the need for specific change, but only once real trust has been established, so your challenge is not just more unwelcome feedback. This means working from a place of unconditional positive regard at all times. It means also choosing the right moment to challenge.

Pitfalls

- Acting as an advocate for the organization with a brief to persuade your client to change.
- Staying blind yourself to the choices your client may have.
- Offering explanations of what is going on from your desire to problem solve.
- Directly challenging at the wrong moment and creating dissonance/mistrust.

Bibliography

Beckhard, R. and Harris, R. (1987) *Organizational Transitions: Managing Complex Change*, Reading, MA: Addison-Wesley Publishing Company.

80

Question of the week

Mags McGeever

Purpose

This strategy uses the power of the unconscious mind to assist the client in making shifts in their thinking to enable them to move forward.

Description

The unconscious mind is incredibly powerful. Having set it a question, even while the conscious mind is thinking about what to make for dinner, the unconscious mind may be considering the question; turning it over, looking at it from different angles and ultimately finding a fresh perspective of great use to the client. In some circumstances, the question does not even need to be explicitly answered. Merely setting it may cause changes in the client's behaviour and outlook. It can be very enlightening for a client when they realize the depth of awareness and new perspectives that can be gained by doing something so easy. It is simply a question of trusting in the process . . . as well as setting a good question!

A good way to use this strategy would be to set a question during the coaching session for consideration by the client in the period before the next session. A question of the week (QOTW)!

Process

- Towards the end of a session and taking the lead from the most significant issue raised therein, a QOTW may be set. This may be done by either the coach or the client. A useful approach is for the coach to set the question for a few weeks until the client becomes familiar with the process, at which point they may be keen to set their own question. On occasion it might be helpful to do some questioning around a client-set QOTW to make sure it is relevant and sufficiently challenging.
- You can then elicit some ideas from the client for keeping the QOTW in mind throughout the week. This might be by visual prominence (e.g. a note on the fridge/a post-it note on the bathroom mirror/a screensaver) or more subtle methods for those who prefer to keep their QOTW private (e.g. to repeat the QOTW each time they brush their teeth/ to consider the QOTW whenever they eat).
- Do highlight to the client that they do not need to consciously answer the QOTW. So, for example, while they are brushing their teeth they may just want to ask themselves the question. They do not need to try to answer it.
- In the following session you may ask the client about things related to the QOTW. It will be interesting to notice any progress made by the client in areas where they previously felt stuck or confused. Or indeed any changes of attitude that have allowed them to take a course of action they previously felt was unavailable to them.
- Some clients enjoy having a notebook reserved exclusively for their QOTWs and any responses to them that they may have noted.

Pitfalls

It is difficult to prove the power of the unconscious mind. Clients who are not familiar or comfortable with this may doubt the efficacy of this exercise and be reluctant to take part. For many years they will have been trained that if you want to find a solution you need to really focus on the issue and think HARD. They might think that this process is too easy to be worthwhile.

Bibliography

Fonagy, P. and Target, M. (2002) *Psychoanalytic Theories: Perspectives from Developmental Psychopathology*, Hoboken, NJ: Wiley-Blackwell.

81

Raising awareness at the start of a coaching relationship – using 360-degree feedback

Heather Cooper

Purpose

This strategy, used at the start of a coaching relationship, aims to identify the coachee's current performance levels by gathering 360-degree feedback. By collating and feeding back this information, the coachee gains a more accurate view of their levels of performance than just their own self-perceptions.

Description

Some coaches conduct diagnostic interviews over the telephone or have a number of face-to-face meetings at the beginning of a coaching relationship. To find a less time-consuming solution, a number of web-based questionnaires have been designed, which focus on specific areas of performance linked to the coaching objectives that often crop up such as leadership, personal impact or influencing styles. These web-based questionnaires are circulated to the coachee, their subordinates, peers and superiors. The system collates the results into a report and this is fed back to the coachee.

Process

The results are often fed back at the beginning of the coaching programme and the following approach used:

- **Step 1 (when working with a coachee's leadership style)**
  Discuss recent leadership theories. Ask the coachee about their beliefs about leadership – what aspects of leadership do they admire or reject and why?
- **Step 2**
  Ask the coachee who they chose to complete the report, and how they thought they might be seen by their respondees. How would they rate themselves as a leader?
- **Step 3**
  Review the feedback and discuss the findings.
- **Step 4**
  Agree actions and next steps.

Pitfalls

- Respondees might not be honest in their feedback (although with enough respondees it is easy to see a pattern emerging).
- Some 360-degree questionnaires can be overly complex.
- Coachees might not initially recognize the feedback they are receiving and can be defensive.

Bibliography

Cooper, H. (2009) 'Using 360-degree feedback improves self awareness', *Coaching at Work*, 3(6): 10.

82

Stakeholder mapping for success and influence

Christine K. Champion

Purpose

The purpose of this strategy is to deepen understanding of the impact an individual has on others.

Description

Recognizing that all executives need strong, positive working relationships with a range of people within and outside their organization, this exercise helps to identify key stakeholders and to provide an action plan for positive influence. Often, individuals have their own agendas and special concerns and seek to protect their vested areas of interest. We hear about the silo-mentalities within functional business areas, which serve to separate, divide and work against the best interests of the organization. The identification of key stakeholders can help to remove boundaries within the organization, a clear benefit, and can also support the career development and promotion of the client.

Process

There are a number of ways to produce a stakeholder map. A wheel can be divided into segments and labelled with stakeholder information, or this can be presented in a hierarchical chart format. It can also be insightful to plot each person/group on a 2 × 2 matrix to assess the relative level of power and influence. Draw out your network/power map and consider how each identified person can help you with your objectives. Be specific and develop a plan to connect. Look for any gaps and consider how to draw in additional supporters. Beware of people who may have their own agendas and may want to hold you back. Consider working with a key 'mentor' and be specific about what you would like to gain from the relationship. Ensure that you make your goals transparent. Review your progress against your objectives. Questions to ask:

- Whose support do you need the most to succeed with your objectives?
- What politics are at play?
- Who are your personal champions?
- How can you check out your assumptions about support and opposition?
- How can you leverage inside–outside links?
- How can these identified stakeholders support you in your future priorities and challenges?
- What tactics will you use to engage each stakeholder?

Pitfalls

The drawing of the stakeholder map will provide real insight into the nature of key stakeholders but without action to move forward against personal objectives it will limit any potential for development. Gaining commitment to future actions and reviewing the impact of this will provide the real momentum.

Bibliography

Garavan, T. N. (1995) 'Stakeholders and strategic human resource development', *Journal of European Industrial Training*, 19(10): 11–16.

83

The Daisy Model: a framework to generate a vision of who the coachee strives to be as a successful professional

Elspeth Campbell

Purpose

The Daisy Model from Coordinated Management of Meaning theory is a conceptual framework to explore with the client the construction of her/his professional identity and ask systemic circular questions because the quality of the question you ask determines the quality of the response.

Description

This is an exercise where you facilitate the client in identifying the elements of his/her professional identity. Through asking quality questions, the client becomes clearer on what makes up success.

Process

Before you start the exercise, invite the client to draw a circle with a number of petals so the result looks like a daisy.

Step 1: Centre of the daisy

At the start, evoke the client's account of professional success, in order to assess how they construct their identity as a professional. This line of inquiry brings to connected consciousness professional experiences along a time line from recent past to future. In seeking a description of a core professional action that expresses success for your client try asking:

- Tell me a story about when you have felt most successful, or
- Tell me a story of a crisis or challenge where you made things come right.

If the client is feeling particularly depleted, it could be difficult to find something for which s/he feels successful at the moment and so success in any area of their life can be evoked.

Next, steps 2–8 map contextual influences on the account of success by inquiry, which invites scripts and stories, as indicated below in each petal of the daisy. The conceptual model is intended to be used as a flexible framework in that all or some of the scripts and stories may be explored or not, each in more or less depth than the others, according to what feels appropriate. The questions suggested below would be adapted by the coach to use the specific language and terms that fit their coachee's context.

Relational script

Who else does your success matter to – colleagues, peers, stakeholders – and whose opinion do you respect the most? Let's draw a stakeholder map . . .

Organization culture story

What was going on in the organization at the time that enabled your key suggestions to be heard?

Professional identity script

You seem to give much thought to how you acted in those circumstances. I wonder if there is a moral or ethical consideration for you here, perhaps shared by others in your profession?

Managerial script

What do you usually believe as a manager you must do when that . . . happens?

Personal identity story

How would you talk about yourself differently now, here, if you hadn't had this success?

Family script

Who were the key people in your family who influenced who you are now as a professional? Let's draw a genogram briefly . . .

Socio-economic environment story

What was going on outside the organization that made success like this, internally, unique?

Concluding step

A summary may be appropriate where the coach shares her/ his interpretative ideas by showing the information from the daisy and asking: 'Now that you know this about yourself, what more can you do?'.

Benefits

When asking circular questions to explore these contextual stories or beliefs we create an enriched description of the account of success, which builds a cameo within each petal of the daisy flower so that, when viewed in its entirety, the picture of the coachee's capacity for success becomes embossed with embellished meaning. It may take a few coaching sessions to complete this inquiry and some reflection by the coach between coaching sessions will assist the evolving picture.

Bibliography

Cronen, V. E. (1992) 'Coordinated management of meaning: theory for the complexity and contradictions of everyday life', in Siegfried, J. (ed) *The Status of Common Sense in Psychology*, Norwood, NJ: Ablex.

84

The Meta Model

Bruce Grimley

Purpose

The purpose of the Meta Model is to help an individual more fully understand the meaning of the language they use. It does this by asking the well-known what, when, who, where and how questions. The purpose of these questions is to help an individual use their language so it accurately represents exactly what they are thinking about at a deeper level. This has the effect of connecting the individual's language with their sensory experience; this in turn creates greater clarity and therefore satisfaction in communicating, both for the speaker and for the listener.

Description

The Meta Model is a collection of 13 syntactic patterns in human speech along with the appropriate challenges. It is a model about another model, and that model is language. In the short space here it is not possible to go through each pattern so I have outlined a coaching strategy that uses the principles of the Meta Model and works very well.

Process

1 Establish rapport.
2 Listen very carefully to *every* word the other person says.
3 As you listen to each word, run an internal video in your

head so you can translate each word into an aspect of that video.

4 When you find you cannot run the video because there is a word that does not translate into 'video format', find a what, when, who, where or how question to uncover the information. Often, these will be abstract words like 'angry'. An appropriate question would be 'how do you *know* they are angry?'.

5 Ensure you retain rapport and pace the other person's current map of the world as you ask each question.

You are likely to find that the individual will start to use language with greater accuracy.

Pitfalls

• If you do not establish rapport when using Meta Model questions you will appear inquisitorial and the coaching will be counterproductive.

• After asking some Meta Model questions there may be a temptation to begin to guess at what the other person means, or where the dialogue is taking them. At these times, stick to the Meta Model questions and allow the emergent meanings to become apparent to the other person at their pace.

• Do not start using Meta Model questions *too soon* in a conversation. Make sure that a good rapport, using matching and pacing skills, is built up first.

• Meta Model questions are powerful and the other person may need time to answer them. Do not rush them as they search for an appropriate answer. Allow them all the time they need. Practise being silent as they do this and learn to be comfortable with these silences.

• Do not ask multiple Meta Model questions; this will only confuse the other person.

Bibliography

Bandler, R. and Grinder, J. (1975) *The Structure of Magic*, Palo Alto, CA: Science and Behaviour Books.

85

Try an experiment:
what happens when you try

Joan O'Connor

Purpose

This technique is particularly useful when someone is concerned or worried about not being able to get the 'right'
outcome first time or when trying out an activity that is new
or outside their comfort zone.

Description

This strategy encourages the client to experiment and so to
reduce the risk of failure. You work with the client to focus
on an issue by taking one step at a time.

Process

Set up the activity as an exploration, looking at what happens when they do the activity. First, ask the person to talk
to you about what outcome they want and how they want to
achieve it. Agree the outcome and actions with the person.
Identify the first action to take and ask them to focus only on
this one. Tell them to treat the activity as an experiment:
their objective is to notice what happens when they carry
out the action: 'When you do x, what happens?'. Ask them to
record the information and also any reactions or thoughts
they have about it. Ask them to bring the information to the
next conversation with you so that you can review it.

People often think they have to go from A to Z in one
step. By focusing on the first action only it helps them realise

that they can take a step-by-step approach and move to the next stage when they are comfortable to do so.

By setting the task as an experiment, there is no right or wrong answer, and the activity is framed as a learning activity. It is simply information to explore, review and learn from.

Example

Jane found it difficult to initiate conversations with colleagues unless it was work related. She wanted to be able to engage with people on a more personal level, but the idea filled her with dread. We identified someone she felt comfortable to approach and also had a work reason to talk about. Jane's task was to ask this person about how their weekend had been before moving into the work topic. Her objective was to notice how the person responded and pay attention to her own reactions as well.

At our next meeting, Jane reported that the conversation had gone well: her colleague had responded with lots of information and they discovered areas of common interest. By the end of the conversation they had agreed to have lunch to discuss the work topic in more detail. Jane said that being able to see the task as an experiment enabled her to relax more, which allowed the conversation to flow more easily. She had noticed she felt less apprehensive and less awkward in approaching her colleague.

Pitfalls

A coachee may continue to be reluctant to take the first step of action. The coach may need to spend more time exploring what is stopping them and help them break this down into small, positive steps.

Bibliography

MacKewn, J. (1997) *Developing Gestalt Counselling*, London: Sage Publications.

86

Understanding how previous life experiences have impacted on the client and the connection to the behavioural patterns they demonstrate today

Heather Cooper

Purpose

This is a strategy that is used to deepen a client's under-standing of how their previous life experiences impact on their behaviour today.

Description

The coaching assumption or belief is that by deepening the client's self awareness, they have a greater capacity to make fundamental shifts in their behaviour. Clients can assess whether their patterns are still in service to them (i.e. are they still helpful?) or whether certain behaviours result in difficulties for them. It is also a great way for clients to stand back and think about where they are going, either personally or in their careers. Typically, as a result of completing this exercise, clients find it easy to see where the 'pathway' is leading.

An influence that underpins this strategy comes from the work performed by life coaches. Life coaching can be focused: where the client is encouraged to set targets and a series of actions to help them reach their goals. The actions will be a step-by-step approach, leading towards their achieving their goals. This suggests that one can influence one's direction in life, rather than allowing events to dictate one's future. Here are the simple steps for building this self awareness.

Process

- **Step 1**
  Using a flip chart or a wipe board, ask the client to draw a path or time line from left to right and plot the most significant events throughout their life, leaving a section blank at the end of the path to represent their future.
- **Step 2**
  Ask the client to talk each event through, asking why they chose that particular event, why it was significant to them and what that event/choice says about them. For example, if the client had highlighted a strong academic track record they may say that they have a strength in analysis or creative writing, or that they enjoy research, or that they are driven to achieve a high standard of academic performance.
- **Step 3**
  Start with the earliest experiences, moving forward to the present day, and record comments the client makes. Once you have reviewed their 'pathway', look at the comments you have noted and ask the client to summarize their talents and typical behaviours.
- **Step 4**
  Review the exercise and ask questions such as:

  - What are the main themes that have emerged for you?
  - What have you learnt about yourself?
  - What would others say about you?
  - How do these patterns of behaviour play out for you currently?
  - How do you believe that these patterns of behaviour will play out for you in the future?

Behaviour is formed by focusing on strong empathy, listening deeply to what is being said and unsaid and the use of appreciative enquiry to build deeper self awareness for the coachee. Often, the 'pathway' reveals both highs and lows regarding the client's personal makeup and can lead to deep developmental conversations. You have to be careful not to steer the conversation but allow this journey of self discovery to emerge.

Pitfalls

Make sure that the client states their own conclusions and beware of your own projections on any particular event, for example that a strong academic track record must mean you were a swot at school!

Bibliography

Cooperrider, D. L. and Whitney, D. (1999) *Collaborating for Change: Appreciative Inquiry*, San Francisco, CA: Barrett-Koehler Communications.

87

Using metaphors to unlock your thinking

Joan O'Connor

Purpose

People are often unaware how much they talk in metaphors to describe their thoughts and feelings in everyday conversation. In a coaching capacity, asking your coachee to describe their issue or thoughts in this way can help to unlock their thinking and provide new insights.

Description

This exercise gets the client to use a metaphor as a way of describing a situation or issue. The process generates insights.

Process

Ask your coachee to describe the issue/situation as an object or image. Ask them to describe the object/image as fully as possible. Use prompt questions such as:

- What can you see?
- What shape is the object?
- What size is it?
- What colour is it?
- What is it doing?

Usually, thinking of the issue/situation in this way provides new insight for the coachee. Once they have finished exploring the object, ask them to think about the issue again and establish whether their thoughts are different in any way. Explore this information with them to help them look at the situation from a new or different perspective. To move them forward into action, ask them how the new information can help to resolve the situation.

Example

Clare was keen to be promoted but felt that her boss didn't always take her seriously. In exploring the reasons for this she thought she was maybe giving mixed messages but wasn't sure how she was doing this. I asked Clare to think about the situation and think of an image that represented it. 'It's like being a set of those Russian dolls; sometimes I'm the big doll, sometimes I'm the little one.' This information enabled Clare to examine how she behaved in different situations with her boss and to create an action plan for being more assertive in some of them.

Pitfalls

- Some people find it difficult to work with metaphors; therefore this approach may not work for them.
- New insights often have a powerful effect and a coachee may need some time to adjust to or digest the new information. Initially, they may also be concerned that they don't know what to do with the insight, for example how to move to action. The coaching may need to help the coachee work through these concerns before the individual is ready to move to action.

Bibliography

MacKewn, J. (1997) *Developing Gestalt Counselling*, London: Sage Publications.

88

Using words to connect with thoughts and feelings

Joan O'Connor

Purpose

Sometimes the words we use can give insights to thoughts and feelings that we have about an issue. Often we can be using certain word(s) consistently and not be aware of doing so. Playing these back to the coachee can help them to reflect on and connect to the thoughts and feelings that go with what they have said.

Description

This exercise focuses on the specific words a client uses. When a word occurs often, you invite the client to explore what that might mean.

Process

When you notice your coachee using words consistently, point this out to them: 'I've noticed that you have mentioned [word] several times, are you aware of this? Tell me more about what this word means for you'. This enables the coachee to reflect on and consider the thoughts or feelings associated with the word.

Example

Mike wanted to build his profile within his organization but was struggling to talk about his strengths and achievements.

I asked him to talk about some of the work projects he had been responsible for. As he talked about different ones, I noticed that the word 'inefficiency' kept coming up. I pointed this out to him and asked him to tell me more about his thoughts on inefficiencies. This led to a discussion on how he really enjoyed being able to seek out change and improvements within his areas of responsibility and also that he saw this as a vital component of a manager's role. He hadn't made this connection previously and realized that this was something he felt strongly about.

Pitfalls

Sometimes people are not consciously aware that they are using a specific word, or why they use that word, it may take them some time to be able to recognize the reasons (cognitive or emotional). This will require the coach to remain patient and curious, helping the person explore the reasons.

89

When the coach or client gets stuck

Darryl Stevens

Purpose

The purpose of this exercise is to help the coaching client and the coach explore the reasons why they are finding themselves stuck in a coaching session and unable to move forward.

Description

The irony of getting stuck in a coaching session is that it can be useful. Many coaches have shared with me their fear of not knowing what to do or ask next. It can also indicate a lack of engagement, boredom or confusion. For the client who becomes stuck, it can be a frustrating and difficult place and may be represented by feeling blocked, lost or overwhelmed for example. Whatever the reason or feeling associated with not knowing what to do next, the first step is to recognize it.

Process

When the client becomes stuck, be patient, give them space and remain comfortable with where you have arrived. Stay silent but present as they assimilate where they are and process their thoughts. Should you feel that a coaching intervention is required, ask them: 'What's happening for you right now?'. Re-enforce their feelings and thoughts by mirroring their language and summarizing what they are describing. Be curious with any metaphoric references, for example: I am cornered; I have hit a brick wall; I am swimming in toffee. Also observe any relevant body language – are they sitting in a twisted position, sighing or shaking their head. By making this known to the client and asking if it has any significance to the situation, it will encourage any important subconscious realities to be revealed.

Allow the agenda to be controlled by your client so that it remains their agenda, encouraging them to find their own solutions. As thoughts are verbalized, you may choose to ask, 'What do you want to do with this?' or 'What would be useful now?'. When they are ready to progress, this is where the shift can take place and having experienced the pain of being stuck, the derived pleasure and sustainability of their choices as they more forward are often more profound.

If you as the coach reach a point of uncertainty or one of feeling stuck, access the signals that are telling you this, choosing your timing to express what is happening for you. The strategy 'Managing yourself during the coaching session' on p. 55 explains how to do this. Such awareness is a powerful compliment to that which the client is experiencing themselves.

Pitfalls

Human beings tend to avoid feelings of discomfort where possible and so in staying with them, albeit with the support of a coach, the client can find it intense and draining. They may therefore choose not to explore this occurrence for too long, if at all. Remain mindful of this and do not force the situation. When you do work through a place of challenge with your client, be aware that it can also be a stressful process for an intuitive coach. Position your feedback and self analysis in a tailored way according to the client you are coaching and the nature of the session. It takes courage to use this strategy but, when applied effectively, it brings real value to the client in identifying progressive strategies to overcome the sticking point.

90

Work/life balance: changing life habits

Penny Swinburne

Purpose

People are often aware of a general dissatisfaction with 'the way things are' – spending too much time working, things they would like to do that they don't have time for. This exercise was originally designed to help working women achieve a work/life balance nearer to their desired one. With the current pressures of 24/7, it has a potentially much wider audience.

Description

The exercise helps the client think about the reality behind their work/life balance. It raises awareness of what their current situation actually is, what they would really like it to be, supported by developing strategies to bring about the change. It can convert a generalized dissatisfied feeling to a clearer perception of what is at the root of this and whether it's worth the effort to change it. It can also lead to someone accepting that they do some things really because they want to, although it feels like an 'ought'.

Process

Ask the client to draw a circle. This is then divided into three segments, representing roughly in size the amount of time they spend in: paid work (W), home life (H) and leisure (L). W, H and L are written on the relevant segments. This first circle represents life **as it is now**. The client then draws a second circle of the same size, similarly divided into three segments, but representing their life **as they would like it to be**.

In deciding what goes where, H are activities that have to be done, but are not particularly pleasurable to the person – they would not miss them if they did not do them. L are pleasurable activities. For example, gardening may be in H for some if they do it just to avoid a mess and in L for others because they really enjoy gardening.

If someone is *highly stressed* by some activities that leave them little energy for other things, it's useful to rephrase the exercise as *'how much time and energy'* is spent in each of the three segments.

Once the diagrams are completed, the coach can help with (a) awareness raising, by asking questions around what is in each segment and (b) developing strategies to move the current situation towards the desired proportions. Useful questions include:

- What's in the H/L segment at the moment?
- What else would you like to be in the L segment?
- How would it feel if you could change it?
- On a scale of 1 to 10, how important would it be to you to change it?

For the H (and W) segments:

- Who else could do it?
- What would happen if? (it wasn't done, someone else did it etc)
- Replace the statement 'I have to' with 'I want to'. How does that feel?

Pitfalls

Naturally detailed thinkers may start analyzing their days hour by hour, including time spent sleeping and where this fits. It helps to emphasize that this is not so much a time log, but about how life feels to them in time/energy and satisfaction terms.

Bibliography

McMahon, G. (2005) *No More Anxiety: Be Your Own Anxiety Coach*, London: Karnac Books.

1

When a client gets stuck

91

Being stuck is part of the creative process

Gill Dickers

Purpose

The purpose of this exercise is to generate options using a creative process.

Description

The impulse to create is one of our most basic impulses. In creativity there is a process and an end product. The process demands courage, will, originality and preseverance. By writing an essay, or completing a project, people are engaging in a creative process that will have an end product, which will be publicly graded. Not surprisingly, students often get overwhelmed by this process. By having too much, or too little information, they run out of time, cannot see the wood for the trees, cannot face the blank page, or cannot think clearly: they are temporarily stuck. This activity recognizes that being stuck is part of the creative process. Materials required are flip chart paper, blue tack, felt tips and gentle music.

Process

As Gordon (1975), suggests, being stuck is a stage of incubation and vital to the process of creativity. In my experience, the creative mind is more likely to be released and solutions found if we allow ourselves to play, by getting on the floor and drawing with colour on large sheets of paper. Visual learners enjoy working in this way, as do many other learners who feel blocked. It is also fun, and learning happens more readily when people enjoy themselves. Non-intrusive music supports this process. The exercise also recommends some familiarity with neuro-linguistic programming (NLP) techniques as discussed by O'Connor and Lages (2002).

I have identified three steps for this strategy:

1 Visualizing both being stuck and being unstuck

If your client is finding the process of writing an essay or completing a project difficult, ask them to divide the flip chart paper vertically into two. On one half they should draw an image of how they are now; on the other, how they imagine they will be when the work is completed, when the problem is solved. In NLP this is called the 'desired state'. They should spend some time considering the feelings created by both images and write these under each image.

2 Blue sky

Ask your student or client to have a blue sky moment, where they talk about all possible ways in which they could move to the desired state. These can be sketched at the top of the sheet, using either words or images. For example, asking for help could be an option. A picture of a tutor or line manager would summarise the idea. Positive and negative consequences of each option should be explored and one or two options chosen.

3 Decisions and action

To conclude, ask the student or client to record what their chosen options are, and when they are going to take action. Then check out their commitment to take action.

Pitfalls

Working in this way can be threatening if participants are primarily auditory learners, or if they are not comfortable with using visual media and colour.

Bibliography

Gordon, R. (1975) 'The creative process: self-expression and self-transcendence', in Jennings, S. (ed) *Creative Therapy*, London: Pitman Press.

O'Connor, J. and Lages, A. (2002) *Coaching with NLP: A Practical Guide to Getting the Best Out of Yourself and Others*, London: Element, HarperCollins.

92

Get out of your head and into your body

Caroline Shola Arewa

Purpose

This strategy shifts the focus of attention from the head to the body with the aim of helping people clear their minds and create space in order to develop clarity. It works well if people arrive at a session flustered with things they don't want to interfere with the coaching session. It can be used effectively when clients are feeling stuck and overwhelmed. At times people tend to overcomplicate matters by trying too hard and not allowing any spontaneity or deeper expression to come through. Sometimes things just get too heady!

Description

The technique works as a kind of human *defragmentation*. Defragmentation is a computer program that clears space on a hard drive. It gets rid of any unnecessary programmes and documents that are causing the system to go slow. Likewise, shifting attention from the cognitive to the kinaesthetic helps people slow down a bit, releases confusion and creates space in the mind. As a result, people feel more clarity and be less stuck. It is an opportunity to shift energy and clear the mind. The coach can also use the strategy if they feel stuck when coaching.

Process

Invite your client *to get out of their head and into their body*. I suggest that you, as coaches, do the technique with your client, so clients feel supported. Identify a time when a shift in energy is required and ask your client: 'Would it help to take a moment to refocus?'. Assuming they say yes, continue by inviting them to move. Use some or all of the following suggestions:

- Stand up and take a moment to stretch.
- Deepen your breath.
- Rotate your neck in both directions to release any tension.
- Rotate your shoulders to release tightness.
- Stretch your spine in all directions.
- Rotate your wrists and ankles.
- Finish by asking your client: 'Is there is anything else your body needs?'.
- They may then make a few more movements.

Pitfalls

- There are no contra-indications to these instructions as they allow clients to stretch within their own movement range.
- Kinaesthetic tools can be powerful. It is important, however, that the coach feels comfortable and confident from experience of working with the body. If the coach feels at all awkward, it can transfer to the client.
- Clients may feel a bit silly at first, a sign that they are moving out of the head!

Bibliography

Arewa, C. S. (2003) *Embracing Purpose, Passion and Peace*, London: Inner Vision Books.

93

Helping a coachee to become 'unstuck'

Heather Cooper

Purpose

This is a strategy used when coachees notice themselves going round and round in circles with a particular issue or typical behavioural pattern, which undermines their effectiveness.

Description

Expressing feelings as they happen with a client underpins the coaching model. This technique is inspired by the Gestalt approach where the whole of a person's experience is considered important: thoughts, feelings and body sensations. The Gestalt approach focuses on the 'here and now' – what is happening moment by moment. Staying with present experience allows the coachee to become more aware. 'Unfinished business' from the past that causes fixed ways of being can emerge and be completed. Different aspects of one's own self come into awareness, allowing more fulfilling relationships and a freer way of functioning in the world.

In its simplest terms, the cycle of awareness (highlighted by Fritz Perls, the founder of Gestalt therapy; see Houston, 1995) has three stages:

1 sensation (noticing emotions, energy, fear, for example);
2 contact (the point at which an individual is mobilized to do something);

3 withdrawal (the point at which the individual is satisfied and moves on to the next cycle of awareness).

When the cycle is interrupted, a charge of residual energy remains, perhaps tensions or anxiety. By continuing to raise awareness of the sensation, the coachee can become more self aware, so work towards contact and eventually withdrawal.

Gestalt is a philosophy of being in the world. For this reason, there are no prescribed methodologies. Instead, the coach embraces the philosophy and creates their methods within that. The step-by-step process shown below illustrates my typical way of using Gestalt.

- **Step 1**

  Ask the coachee what they would like to work on.
- **Step 2**

  As the coachee describes the issue, notice your own reactions and listen deeply to what is said, unsaid, body language, mannerisms, choice of language, tone, etc.
- **Step 3**

  Notice your own sensations in response to the coachee. Share your sensations as a vehicle for the coachee to share their own sensations. Encourage the coachee to raise their level of awareness of their sensations. Remember that the goal of the coach is to raise awareness moment by moment, rather than problem solving or putting structure into the conversation.
- **Step 4**

  If the coachee gets stuck, ask them to draw the situation on paper or use other imagery such as metaphors or similes. Stay with the unknown or the dilemma.
- **Step 5**

  As the level of awareness grows, the coachee makes contact or has a moment of realization about their behaviour. With the insight, the coachee has choices and is mobilized into action.
- **Step 6**

  At this stage, be creative about different choices. Think the unthinkable before deciding on a course of action.

Pitfalls

Working with Gestalt can be incredibly powerful and transformational intervention. However, you can easily slip into
problem solving. Gestalt is a way of 'being' with clients,
thereby the coach needs to focus and express emotional
responses and feelings with the client as they work together.

Bibliography

Houston, G. (1995) *Red Book of Gestalt*, London: Rochester
    Foundation.

94

Recognize and release fear

Caroline Shola Arewa

Purpose

This simple yet powerful strategy is usefully implemented when a client is stuck and finding it difficult to progress. Clients often suffer with a common disease known as excusitis! You may have had it yourself where there seems to be no logical way forward. Obstacles present themselves everywhere you turn. This disease has one main cause – fear!

Description

This easy to use strategy inspires people to move beyond fear. It consists of an exploration of what fear is and how it arises, an acronym and a power question to get people unstuck and moving forward.

Process

Fear is the cause of a multitude of problems. It often shows up as procrastination, creativity blocks, poor self-esteem, lack of clarity and can even show itself in physical illness. Instead of moving through life, facing issues, *if* and *when* they arise, people often create issues in the mind and then behave as if they are real. It is said that most people worry about things that will never ever happen!

Fear has been defined as: **F**alse **E**vidence **A**ppearing **R**eal or **F**orget **E**verything **A**nd **R**un. Does that sound familiar to you or your clients? We respond to things that have not occurred, and will not occur. Fear is the gap between failure and success. Even if we are 70 per cent toward success, it will not be enough to bridge the gap. Will Rogers said: 'Even if you are on the right track you will get run over if you just sit there.' To succeed we must be 110 per cent prepared to release fear and reach for success. The simplest way is to replace fear with faith.

When fear is preventing action, ask clients to answer the following power question: 'If I were not so afraid I would?'. This frees the imagination. If clients reply saying 'but I can't', simply invite them to *act as if they can*. Again, this releases fear and frees the imagination.

If necessary, continue to repeat the original question until you get a result.

Pitfalls

There are no pitfalls, only the potential to move beyond fear and take massive action.

Bibliography

Arewa, C. S. (2003) *Embracing Purpose, Passion and Peace*, London: Inner Vision Books.

Collins, R. (Ed.) (1992) *Will Rogers Says: Favorite Quotations by the Will Rogers Memorial Staff*, Oklahoma City, OK: Neighbors and Quaid.

95

Reframing

Julia Cusack

Purpose

The purpose of this strategy is to allow the client to think differently about a situation that is preoccupying them or a situation where they are stuck.

Description

This is a challenging exercise to help people see a seemingly intractable situation from another perspective. It allows them to be creative about the possibility of another interpretation to their story. It also increases their ownership of the situation and allows them to face and discharge their emotions in a logical and systematic way. It gets them right to the heart of the situation and helps to direct them effectively towards actions for handling it differently next time.

Process

1 Your client tells you their story about the situation, for example: 'I am so angry with her. She was just sitting there doing nothing while Sandy just trampled all over our work. She didn't back me up at all; that's her all over, selfish and cowardly. She knew I needed backup at that point and it's just typical of her not to stand up for what's right'.
2 List in a column, on (preferably) a flip chart or white board, the component parts of the story the client has told.

3 Then ask them if each statement is true, false or they don't know.
4 Finally, ask them what they **do** know to be true about each situation.

Table 6 provides a worked example.

Table 6 **Reframing exercise**

Story	True, false or don't know	Reframe
I am so angry with her	True, I *am* angry, although it is my anger, not literally *with* her	I am angry
She was just sitting there doing nothing	False – she was breathing, listening, watching, thinking, moving her hands	I couldn't see a reaction from her
While Sandy trampled all over our work	False – she didn't *trample* it, Sandy presented the work we'd been asked to do in the way she thought it should be done	She didn't acknowledge our contribution or our effort
She didn't back me up at all	Don't know – she may have been backing me up silently; she may have backed me up after the meeting	She didn't intervene publicly at the time
That's her all over, selfish and cowardly	False – she is not selfish and cowardly 'all over'	I don't like the way she behaved at that point
She knew I needed backup at that point	Don't know – she may have, she may not; she may have realized later	I wanted her to back me up. I didn't ask for backup but I could have

And it's just typical of her not to stand up for what's right	False – it may be typical of her not to stand up for what I think is right but she may have been standing up for what she thought was right	I am frustrated that at that moment I wasn't able to stand up in an effective way for what I think is right

Pitfalls

It can take people some time to realize that their stories are rarely 'true'. They may well argue back so this exercise can take some persistence. However, the effort required definitely pays off.

96

Stuck

Aidan Tod

Purpose

The purpose of this strategy is to help clients who are stuck with a powerful belief that some personal attribute or situation is unchangeable, despite their strong desire for it to be changed.

Description

When a client is blocked in thinking or with their emotions it can be really tough trying to find a way forward. It can be really powerful to experiment with physical movement to get the desired mental and/or emotional movement.

Process

If the conversation has highlighted that there is resistance to change yet the client has expressed they want to do something different, suggest an experiment. Keep the explanation brief – perhaps restrict it to something like: 'I can hear you are stuck and I wonder what it would be like if we tried to explore how you might shift your thinking with movement?'. Or: 'I have an idea that might help you – shall we give it a go?'.

First of all, invite the client to stand up and look around the room to become familiar with it. Ask them to go somewhere in the room and find a place where they can feel stuck. Let them do this and then help them to explore their stuckness. What does it feel like to be stuck there? What else might they notice about being in that place? When there is nothing else for them to explore about being stuck, invite them to move to somewhere where they are going to imagine that they are free of the attribute or situation that is preventing them from being as they wish to be.

In the new place ask them to imagine that they no longer have the limiting attribute or situation. 'What is different about you in this place?' 'What do you know in this place that you didn't know in the other?' 'What advice would you give to the person stuck in the other place?' You are likely to notice a change in the individual with more energy and as that happens you might like to ask: 'So what do you need to do now in order to become the person you want to be, or get the outcome you want?'. The client is likely to have some ideas as something will have shifted in them with the specific situation.

Pitfalls

None.

Bibliography

Joyce, P. and Sills, C. (2001) *Skills in Gestalt Counselling and Psychotherapy*, London: Sage Publications.

97

The art of reflective practice

Christine K. Champion

Purpose

This exercise aims to develop independence and resilience. As the 21st century kicks in, we live in a frenetic, action-oriented society, where there are continuous interruptions, and little opportunity for standing back and thinking, or indeed for effective listening – the counterpart of thinking. We are bombarded with information and data from all sides and the challenge is how to make sense of this proliferation of information in order to identify and drive forward the changes that may be required. Often, quick, decisive fire-fighting actions can be taken to the detriment of the longer-term situation. So, it appears that there is little opportunity or indeed encouragement for the activity of reflective practice in business settings. But how can individuals change their behaviours and begin to take time to engage in reflective practice in order to learn from experiences and to take more effective actions for the future?

Description

Reflective practice can be defined as the practice of stepping back to contemplate the meaning of events for ourselves and others. The process illuminates experiences and can provide insights into the basis for considered future actions. Reflective learning is a journey that challenges and questions practice and the established ways of thinking within individuals and organizations. The process encourages frank and

open discussions and debate which surface the social, political and emotional aspects of organizational interactions,
some of which may be blocking operating effectiveness.

This strategy is especially useful in high testosterone
environments where action counts and there is no time to
think.

Process

The coach takes the client through a four-stage process to
reflect in a structured manner on a recent event or a key
issue.

1 Subjective recall of the event – or issue

The first stage is to ask the client to provide an account
from their personal perspective as to what happened:

- What was the event?
- Tell me more about it.
- What did you think/feel?
- How did you react?
- What was it like for you?

2 Objective description

The second stage is to challenge and ask the client to
describe the facts, hard data and other information and to
view the event from a third-party perspective:

- What is really going on here?
- What are the facts?
- Really?
- How might you reframe your earlier statements?
- What does this look like from other key people's
perspectives?
- How else might you view this with all this further hard
information?

3 Critical analysis and evaluation of the event to support
the critical thinking part of the process

- So what is the key meaning in this for you?
- What are the social, political, emotional aspects?

- What stands out for you?
- How do you make sense of all this?

Pitfalls

None.

Bibliography

Schön, D. (1987) *Educating the Reflective Practitioner*, San Francisco, CA: Jossey-Bass.

98

The ball (part 1) and the mud (part 2)

Denis Gorce-Bourge

Purpose

On their way to reach their goals, sometimes people can have a tendency to generalize that their whole life is going wrong and is awful and terrible. It is a very common predicament but, for most of us, these thoughts only last for a few moments or hours. This strategy is useful to go through doubts and fears.

Description

This is a very simple strategy that will help your client get over a moment of crisis or doubt. You will help him/her to realize that the moment is going to pass and that he/she is going to be better very soon because they are capable of resolving the problem themselves. The strategy starts as a metaphor and uses space to put distance between the situation and the person. You will just need a sheet of paper and a pen.

As in many processes, a big goal will often bring doubt and fear at times. The purpose of this strategy is to help people get over a crisis, quickly and easily.

Process

The ball (part 1)

You will know to use this strategy when you hear your client making generalizations or saying, for example, 'It's always the same, everything's going wrong, it is not going to work'. Take a paper and a pen. Ask the person to tell you about which part of his/her life is going wrong. For example:

- What about work?
- Do you have a problem at work?
- Yes? Tell me how big the problem is.

When you have the answer, draw a dot on a piece of paper and ask your client whether the dot is big enough (considering that the entire page is the client's whole life). Ask your client to validate the size of the dot you draw on the piece of paper each time they describe a problem. Keep going for as long as you feel your client has more to say. By the end of this part of the exercise, you will generally have as many dots on the page as your client has problems. Now screw the piece of paper up into a ball. Tell your client that this action is a metaphor for his/her state of mind at the moment. Tell your client, that despite the problems, there are in fact plenty of things that are okay in their life. Unfold the paper, flatten it out and show them that in fact a vast majority of his/her life is going well and that it is not all bad. Ask them to acknowledge this fact and then ask them which problem they want to start working on first.

The mud (part 2)

Ask your client to tell you about a problem they want to work on. Ask them to describe very precisely what they are feeling about the problem and to imagine that there is a small pool of mud surrounding their chair that represents the problem. When your client has clearly expressed what the problem is, ask him/her to get out of the chair and step out of the mud that is surrounding their chair. Tell them to be an observer of this person having this problem (meta-position). Help your client to literally get out of him/herself and to look at him/herself. It can take some time to achieve if he/she has never done it before. Ask your client, as an observer, to tell you what he/she sees, what he/she can do to help, what advice he/she can give to this person having this problem. When you are happy with the advice he/she has for him/herself, ask your client to sit back in the chair and hear the advice. Can he/she hear it? How does he/she feel? Can they see that the mud has dried up or has drained away? Repeat the process as many times as necessary until you get a satisfactory progress in terms of feeling. This strategy can be used separately as 'The ball' (part 1) or 'The mud' (part 2) or together, for maximum results to help a client in a state of doubt.

Pitfalls

None.

99

The presenting issue isn't always the real issue

Peter Melrose

Purpose

Often the coach needs to look beyond the surface performance issue to deeper, underlying issues. The temptation is
often to get into problem solving around the surface issue
instead – and the sponsor may want you to do so. This
strategy is about finding out what is really going on for your
client, which may unlock transformational change.

Description

In this exercise one needs to engage with a client and explore
their underlying feelings, challenges and issues. It is one
where you avoid problem solving and allow the client to
discover the real issues.

Process

Engage first in an exploration of your client's sense of
things. Use open and probing questions and careful listening
to take exploration and understanding deeper. Stay in tune
with your client in this process by reading their level of
energy and engagement. A low level of energy, defensiveness
and confusion are tell-tale signs that the immediate issue
may mask deeper concerns.

Follow your client's own feelings; questioning, challenging, affirming, as necessary. For example, one client who
was seen as difficult and defensive by colleagues had a very

low opinion of her line manager. In exploring this, she said strongly that he did not deserve her compassion. The choice here was to challenge this view or to leave the client to 'sit' with it. Doing the latter is not favoured by problem solvers, but it can be very powerful. Emotions, once surfaced and seen clearly by the client, can have unexpected results. In this case, the client's view had changed by the next session. She found that the act of acknowledging her lack of compassion had shifted her feelings.

Once you find tangible emotion like this, keep it in focus for your client. Ask them to describe the feeling, put it in context with the surface issue, explore its origins and ask what it would be like to feel differently. For example, this same client felt a strong antipathy to her peers. My intuitive sense was that she was boiling inside about something. I asked what was going on for her at that moment. She described a fear of the internal politics and, crucially, of being found out. I detected a new level of disclosure and encouraged her to explore her feelings further. She then revealed for the first time a low self-esteem and a lack of personal fulfillment in her life. This was a breakthrough moment for her to the real underlying issue.

It is important following such breakthrough moments to recontract: agree new, more fundamentally important coaching objectives that reflect the deeper issue. The organization's surface agenda may no longer be immediately in focus, but it is more important to help your client address their own real issues. In that way, clients are most likely to find out how to live up to their potential and do the best they can.

So adjust the focus of enquiry with your client. Above all, keep questioning, listening empathically and affirming your client in what is likely to be new territory for them.

Pitfalls

- Trying to solve the immediate problem.
- Giving up on enquiry too soon.
- Pushing to go deeper than your client wants.
- Offering interpretation and meanings of your own.

Unsticking the stuckness

Julia Cusack

Purpose

The purpose of this strategy is to prompt action when the client is feeling or acting 'stuck'.

Description

People often describe themselves as procrastinators but this is little more than a disempowering label. It is a kind of apathy created by the mind to protect itself. If the client uses words or phrases such as:

- can't be bothered
- I can't
- I don't know
- lazy
- overwhelmed
- stuck
- too tired
- useless

then this strategy is for them. If the activity they are putting off doing feels hard to them, it is a clear indication of resistance. Here's an interesting fact: you can't feel others pushing you, you can only feel yourself pushing back. So it's the client's own resistance that needs to be addressed. Here is a process for helping them let go of their feelings of resistance.

Process

Ask the client questions for the area(s) where they feel stuck, as shown in Table 7.

During the questions, keep probing until they have bottomed out their thoughts and fears around the issue, particularly: 'What's the worst that could happen?'. After this process, check what their next steps are and how they are feeling about the task. You can also suggest they write it down. This serves two purposes. First, it commits it to paper, which makes the 'what would I do?' more likely to happen, and second, the act of reflective writing around the 'worst

Table 7 Unsticking the stuckness exercise

Where I'm stuck	Write my CV and send it to a prospective employer	Write the presentation for the keynote speech
What's the worst that could happen?	They could say: 'That's the worst CV I've ever seen and there's no way I'd give you a job. What on earth were you thinking of, wasting my time?'	I start writing it and realize it's rubbish and have no idea how to proceed and have lost all my confidence and energy
What would be more realistic/likely to happen?	They'd say: 'Thanks for your CV. I'm afraid you don't have the sort of experience we are after'	I would start it, get to a particular point and think it wasn't very good, then be unsure how to continue
How would you feel when the more likely thing happens?	Disappointed. But clear about the level of experience required for that job and my suitability for it	Lost, useless, scared
Then what would you do?	Look for other jobs in the professional magazine and apply for those	Ask a colleague if they would read it and give me some feedback

that could happen' is often very cathartic and can be the key
to unsticking the stuckness.

Pitfalls

None.

When a client is stuck

Heather Cooper

Purpose

Coachees often spend time during sessions grappling with a particular problem that crops up for them regularly. Perhaps there is a particular relationship that they find difficult to deal with or they don't understand why someone else behaves towards them in a particular way. Often the coachee is caught up emotionally in the turmoil and finds it difficult to stand back and look objectively or indeed to look at the situation from different perspectives.

Description

This strategy allows the coachee to stand back from the situation. By acknowledging different views on a problem or situation, the coachee can be more dispassionate and empowered to make shifts in their own behaviour. By acknowledging and owning their own patterns of behaviour and emotional responses paradoxically this can allow change to occur.

Working with coachees in this way is informed partly by Neuro Linguistic Programming (NLP), by Gestalt therapy (the paradoxical nature of change) and by 'chair work'. In particular, the strategy encourages the coachee to notice their behavioural and emotional patterns in these situations, and sometimes to recognise where the root of these patterns come from. By making connections and understanding themselves, coachees can free themselves from limiting thoughts/emotional patterns, to increasing options, creating flexibility and creativity and allowing greater freedom of action.

Process

- **Step 1**
  Ask the coachee to talk through the problem or issue from their perspective. Ask them to notice how they feel emotionally, how they feel physically, and what sense they make of the situations by drawing on different parts of their body.

  - ○ What is the brain saying (accessing their intellectual response)?
  - ○ What is the gut saying (accessing gut feel)?
  - ○ What is the heart saying (accessing their emotional intelligence)?

- **Step 2**
  Ask the coachee to draw a picture of the problem. This encourages the coachee to express themselves using a different medium whilst at the same time distancing themselves from the issue.

- **Step 3**
  The next step is to explore the situation/problem from different positions or perspectives by role playing other people who are engaged in this situation, and to talk from their perspective. The coachee actually changes chair and imagines they are a different party who is involved in the issue and shares their understanding of the problem.

  Coachees can find this hard, but by gentle encouragement and questioning they pick up great insights from actually 'being' the other party. It is import-ant that the coachee speaks as the third party, rather than imagining what they would say. Enrich their understand-ing further by asking the coachee to switch chairs, each time talking from the other individuals' perspective (i.e. fourth party, fifth party, etc.).

- **Step 4**
  Imagine that the room is a time machine where you can

move forward in time and look back on today. Ask the coachee to move to a different place in the room that represents a date sometime in the future and ask them to look back in time to the situation today and describe what they see. This also encourages a dispassionate look at the situation.

- **Step 6**
Ask the coachee to return to their original chair, as themselves, today, to summarize their learning, and consider how they can apply it.

Pitfalls

Take time to explain the exercise and what they are doing at each stage or the coachee could be confused by moving from chair to chair.

Bibliography

Houston, G. (1995) *Red Book of Gestalt*, London: Rochester Foundation.

Knight, S. (2006) *NLP at Work: Neuro Linguistic Programming: The Difference that Makes a Difference in Business*, London: Nicholas Brealey Publishing.

The future

Coaching is a relatively new discipline and, as such, many individuals are becoming engaged in research-based projects aimed at developing an evidence base on what works, with whom and why. Those coaches based in academic establishments are at the forefront of such research. However, as with other disciplines, the more coaches of all types and in all settings that become engaged in the positive outcomes that research can offer, the more the field will develop. The authors would like to encourage coaches of whatever coaching persuasion to embrace research in a bid to think creatively about the many ways in which research can assist those who seek our help. Professional bodies such as the Association for Coaching, the International Coach Federation and the British Psychological Society's Special Group in Coaching Psychology are already actively involved in such research. However, professional bodies are only made up of individuals who hold a wealth of experience and knowledge. Perhaps the challenge for individual coaches is how to become part of the research process, contributing to and learning from the body of growing information and evidence that research offers.

Additional reading materials

Auerbach, J. (2001) *Personal and Executive Coaching: The Complete Guide for Mental Health Professionals*, Ventura, CA: Executive College Press.

Brounstein, M. (2000) *Coaching and Mentoring for Dummies*, New York, NY: Wiley.

Buckley, A. and Buckley, C. (2006) *A Guide to Coaching and Mental Health* (Essential Coaching Skills and Knowledge Series, series eds) McMahon, G., Palmer, S. and Leimon, A., Hove: Routledge.

Burns, D. (1990) *The Feeling Good Handbook*, New York, NY: Plume.

Cavanagh, M., Grant, A. M. and Kemp, T. (2005) *Evidence-Based Coaching: Vol. 1, Theory, Research and Practice from the Behavioural Sciences*, Bowen Hills: Australian Academic Press.

Chapman, T., Best, B. and Van Casteren, P.(2003) *Executive Coaching*, Basingstoke: Palgrave Macmillan.

Cook, M. J. (1999) *Effective Coaching*, New York, NY: McGraw-Hill.

Dryden, W. (2000) *Overcoming Procrastination*, London: Sheldon.

Edgerton, N. and Palmer, S. (2005) 'SPACE: a psychological model for use within cognitive behavioural coaching, therapy and stress management', *The Coaching Psychologist*, 2(2): 25–31. [SPACE Model]

Fitzgerald, C. and Berger, J. G. (2002) *Executive Coaching: Practices & Perspectives*, New York, NY: Davies-Black.

Flaherty, J. (1999) *Coaching: Evoking Excellence in Others*, London: Elsevier.

Fleming, I. and Taylor, A. (1997) *The Coaching Pocketbook*, Alresford: Management Pocketbooks.

Fournies, F. F. (2000) *Coaching for Improved Work Performance* (2nd edition), New York, NY: McGraw-Hill.

Gallwey, W. T. (1975, 1986) *The Inner Game of Tennis*, London: Pan Books in association with Jonathan Cape.

Grant, A. M. (2001) *Towards a Psychology of Coaching*, Sydney: Coaching Psychology Unit, University of Sydney. [Definitions of coaching – article available online]

Grant, A. M. and Greene, J. (2001) *Coach Yourself: Make Real Changes in Your Life*, Harlow: Pearson Education.

Grant, A. M. and Greene, J. (2003) *Solution-Focused Coaching: Managing People in a Complex World*, Harlow: Pearson Education.

Halpern, D. F. (2003) *Thought and Knowledge: An Introduction to Critical Thinking* (4th edition), Mahwah, NJ: Lawrence Erlbaum Associates, Inc.

Harold, F. (2001) *Be Your Own Life Coach*, London: Hodder & Stoughton.

Hauck, P. A. (1991) *Hold Your Head Up High*, London: Sheldon.

Heller, R. (1998) *Managing Change*, London: Dorling Kindersley.

Hindle, T. (1998) *Manage Your Time*, London: Dorling Kindersley.

Honey, P. and Mumford, A. (1982; 3rd edition 1992) *The Manual of Learning Styles*, Maidenhead: Honey Publications.

Isbister, N. and Robinson, M. (1999) *Who Do You Think You Are?*, London: HarperCollins.

Jackson, P. Z. and McKergow, M. (2007) *The Solutions Focus: Making Coaching & Change SIMPLE* (2nd edition), London: Nicholas Brealey. [OSKAR & SIMPLE Models]

Kolb, D. A. (1984) *Experiential Learning: Experience as the Source of Learning and Development*, Upper Saddle River, NJ: Prentice Hall.

Kottler, J. A. (2001) *Making Changes Last*, Philadelphia, PA: Brunner-Routledge.

Leahy, R. (2006) *The Worry Cure*, London: Piatkus.

Lee, G. (2003) *Leadership Coaching: From Personal Insight to Organizational Performance*, London: Chartered Institute of Personnel Development.

Leimon, A., Moscovici, F. and McMahon, G. (2005) *Business Coaching* (Essential Coaching Skills and Knowledge Series, series eds) McMahon, G., Palmer, S. and Leimon, A., Hove: Routledge.

Martin, C. (2001) *The Life Coaching Handbook*, Carmarthen: Crown House Publishing.

McDermott, I. and Jago, W. (2001) *The NLP Coach*, London: Piatkus.

McMahon, G. (2001) *Confidence Works: Learn to Be Your Own Life Coach*, London: Sheldon Press.

McMahon, G. (2005) *No More Anxiety: Learn to Be Your Own Anxiety Coach*, London: Karnac Books.

McMahon, G. (2007) *No More Anger: Be Your Own Anger Management Coach*, London: Karnac Books.

McMahon, G. and Leimon, A. (2008) *Performance Coaching for Dummies*, London: John Wiley.

McMahon, G., Palmer, S. and Wilding, C. (2005) *Achieving Excellence in Your Coaching Practice* (Essential Coaching Skills and Knowledge Series, series eds) McMahon, G., Palmer, S. and Leimon, A., Hove: Routledge.

Megginson, D. and Clutterbuck, D. (2005) *Techniques for Coaching and Mentoring*, Oxford: Butterworth-Heinemann.

Mulligan, E. (1999) *Life Coaching: Change your Life in 7 Days*, London: Piatkus.

Mumford, A. (1995) *Effective Learning*, London: Chartered Institute of Personnel and Development.

Neenan, M. and Dryden, W. (2001) *Life Coaching: A Cognitive-Behavioural Approach*, Hove: Routledge.

Neenan, M. and Palmer, S. (1998) 'A cognitive-behavioural approach to tackling stress', *Counselling*, 9(4): 315–319. [Dual systems model]

Neenan, M. and Palmer, S. (2000) 'Problem focused counselling and psychotherapy', In Palmer, S. (ed) *Introduction to Counselling and Psychotherapy: The Essential Guide*, London: Sage Publications.

Neenan, M. and Palmer, S. (2001) 'Cognitive behavioural coaching', *Stress News*, 13(3): 15–18.

Neenan, M. and Palmer, S. (2001) 'Rational emotive behaviour coaching', *Rational Emotive Behaviour Therapist*, 9(1): 34–41.

Newton, J., Long, S. and Sievers, B. (2006) *Coaching in Depth: The Organizational Role Analysis Approach*, London: Karnac Books.

O'Neill, M. B. (2000) *Executive Coaching with Backbone and Heart*, San Francisco, CA: Jossey-Bass.

Orlick, T. (2000) *In Pursuit of Excellence: How To Win in Sport and Life Through Mental Training* (3rd edition), Leeds: Human Kinetics Europe.

Palmer, S. and Burton, T. (1996) *Dealing with People Problems at Work*, Maidenhead: McGraw-Hill.

Palmer, S. and Cooper, C. (2007) *How to Deal with Stress*, London: Kogan Page. [*Sunday Times* Series]

Palmer, S., Cooper, C. and Thomas, K. (2003) *Creating a Balance: Managing Stress*, London: British Library. [Multimodal coaching]

Parsloe, E. (1999) *The Manager as Coach and Mentor* (2nd edition), London: Chartered Institute of Personnel and Development.

Passmore, J. (2006) *Excellence in Coaching: The Industry Guide*, London: Kogan Page.

Peltier, B. (2001) *The Psychology of Executive Coaching: Theory and Application*, New York, NY: Brunner-Routledge.

Persaud, R. (2005) *The Motivated Mind: How to Get What You Want From Life*, London: Bantam Press.

Prochaska, J. O., DiClemente, C. C. and Norcross, J. C. (1992) 'In search of how people change: applications to addictive behaviors', *American Psychologist*, 47: 1102–1114.

Sperry, L. (2004) *Executive Coaching: The Essential Guide for Mental Health Professionals*, New York, NY: Brunner-Routledge.

Starr, J. (2003) *The Coaching Manual*, London: Prentice Hall.

Stober, D. R. and Grant, A. M. (2006) *Evidence Based Coaching Handbook: Putting Best Practices to Work for your Clients*, Hoboken, NJ: John Wiley.

West, L. and Milan, M. (2002) *The Reflecting Glass: Professional Coaching for Leadership Development*, Basingstoke: Palgrave Macmillan.

Whitmore, J. (1992) *Coaching for Performance*, London: Nicholas Brealey. [GROW model]

Whittaker, M. and Cartwright, A. (2000) *The Mentoring Manual*, Aldershot: Gower.

Whitworth, L., Kimsey-House, H. and Sandahl, P. (1998) *Co-Active Coaching*, Mountain View, CA: Davies-Black.

Williams, P. and Davis, D. C. (2002) *Therapist as Life Coach: Transforming Your Practice*, New York, NY: Norton.

Zeus, P. and Skiffington, S. (2007) *The Complete Guide to Coaching at Work*, Maidenhead: McGraw-Hill Professional.